A Journey in the 4th Dimension

A Primer On Good Living Through Meditation

Chandulal Jivandas Rughani

A Journey in the 4th Dimension
Copyright © 2024 by Chandulal Jivandas Rughani

All rights reserved. No part of this publication may be reproduced, distributed, or transmitted in any form or by any means, including photocopying, recording, or other electronic or mechanical methods, without the prior written permission of the author, except in the case of brief quotations embodied in critical reviews and certain other non-commercial uses permitted by copyright law.

Tellwell Talent
www.tellwell.ca

ISBN
978-1-77941-627-8 (Paperback)

This is my magnum opus, my gift
to the generations to come.

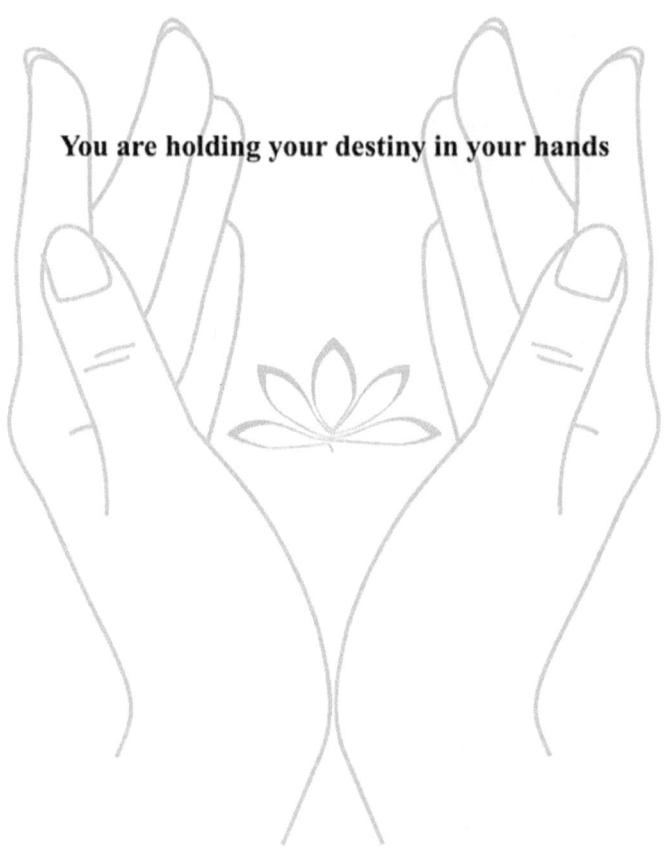

You are holding your destiny in your hands

"There is no wealth like knowledge, and no poverty like ignorance" -Buddha

This book belongs to _____.

It is lent to	on	returned on
_____	__/__/____	__/__/____
_____	__/__/____	__/__/____
_____	__/__/____	__/__/____
_____	__/__/____	__/__/____
_____	__/__/____	__/__/____
_____	__/__/____	__/__/____
_____	__/__/____	__/__/____
_____	__/__/____	__/__/____
_____	__/__/____	__/__/____
_____	__/__/____	__/__/____
_____	__/__/____	__/__/____
_____	__/__/____	__/__/____
_____	__/__/____	__/__/____
_____	__/__/____	__/__/____
_____	__/__/____	__/__/____
_____	__/__/____	__/__/____
_____	__/__/____	__/__/____
_____	__/__/____	__/__/____
_____	__/__/____	__/__/____
_____	__/__/____	__/__/____

TABLE OF CONTENTS

PREAMBLE ix
GRATITUDE xi
PREFACE xv
DISCLAIMER xvii
FOREWARD xix

Part 1: ON THE ROAD…

INTRODUCTION 3
Chapter 1. IMPERMANENCE 11
Chapter 2. LESSONS OF IMPERMANENCE 21
Chapter 3. 5-STAR HOTEL 29
Chapter 4. LES MISÉRABLES 33
Chapter 5. 4-STAR HOTEL 41
Chapter 6. JOIE DE VIVRE 51
Chapter 7. 3-STAR HOTEL 59

Part 2: …THE JOURNEY CONTINUES

Chapter 8. THE MAN, HIS MISSION AND HIS MESSAGE 65
Chapter 9. 2-STAR HOTEL 73
Chapter 10. IMAGINE 77
Chapter 11. 1.5-STAR HOTEL 81
Chapter 12. 1-STAR HOTEL 87
Chapter 13. GROUND ZERO 91
Chapter 14. THE 4TH DIMENSION 95

APPENDIX A 97
APPENDIX B 105
ABOUT THE AUTHOR 107

PREAMBLE

In today's wired world, the incessant demands on people have outstripped the needed congenial assimilation of change over time. Never has there been such a rapid expansion of technology as in this last generation. It continues unabated with tremendous benefits yet taking an unprecedented toll on mental health.

To survive people have to be skilled in relaxation techniques.

This rendition gives some sort of handle to understand the power of meditation. Meditation techniques and the beneficial insights derived from them are not easy to explain. That is why the thrust of meditation to arrest and observe the mind is interweaved with the "science" of the reality (e.g. impermanence) the mind has to deal with. Again, the mind's interaction with the world is very complex, involving consciousness. On top of it all, the insights developed are subjective demanding clarification. Luckily, the writing itself was inspired by doing a lot of meditation!

The in-depth study of the subject requires dedication and perseverance from a serious reader. Also, continuous participation in practicing meditation and logging the analyses empowers the reader with his own insight to tap into the fountain of wisdom.

In today's hectic life, some readers may find solace in it.

May all sentient beings be happy!

GRATITUDE

Over two and a half thousand years ago, there walked a man in the shadows of the Himalayas, who went through a journey to the end of "existence". He later taught the experience of it for the benefit of the human race. From his teachings, he continues to strike a sympathetic cord in anyone who searches for meaning in life. To Siddhartha Gautama, the Buddha, the Enlightened One, I bow down with immense gratitude and reverence.

The Buddha taught that all things, including all "beings", manifest contingent upon various constituents coming together in a timely fashion. Each constituent, in turn, is compounded from other constituents in a similar way, ad infinitum. There is no single independent entity. The making of this book is an example of such a cohesive process; of various people and events conspiring to make it happen. Absence of any one or if an event had happened at a different time, the book would not be same and perhaps would not have existed.

In my search, I came across Vipassana meditation taught by Shree S.N. Goenka, which opened my eyes to the teachings of the Buddha. Apparently, the Buddha's teachings are kept in their pristine purity through generations; to all the monks and nuns, I bestow my heartfelt gratitude. I am particularly grateful to Alain and Rachel Lepine, amongst many assistant teachers, for their guidance. Of course I am indebted to all workers, meditators and drivers sharing rides to the meditation centre.

From time immemorial, human beings have developed communication skills, first to survive amongst other species and then to create language, art, culture and science. There was a time when important ideas were transmitted orally from generation to generation.

With the words later written on a medium of papyrus or clay tablets, wider and sustained exposure was achieved. International exchange of ideas has grown progressively across cultures with the advent of printing and computing technologies. The process of reading and writing is made so easily available. The process of information flow continues! I thank all the entrepreneurs and inventors concerned in various fields of human endeavours to make this book.

My childhood memories with friends have had a profound influence in building my character. The vast base of adventure and camaraderie has set me in good stead for the later years in my journey.

I sincerely respect all my teachers at schools, college and universities, my colleagues and friends, and all whose paths intersected mine to influence me in my endeavours.

I have been blessed to know many people in my activities including volunteering, gym and library; I thank them all.

I pay homage to my parents, who have inculcated spirituality in me. So am I grateful to my ancestors by extension. All my brothers and sisters and their families have contributed in fashioning my ideas. They are always in my thoughts.

Usha, my ex-wife, has given me so much encouragement in this endeavour. My sons, Neel and Ravi, have always supported me. Their partners, Monica and Priya are inspiration personified. Raine, Kamran, Kian, Shaiden and Amar, my grandsons, have added impetus to continue my work. I am thankful to them all.

The late Urania Wolanskyj and families of her daughters, Alexandra and Halyna, had been very supportive in the crucial formative period of writings; my heartfelt gratitude to all. I will always cherish the times we had together. I miss Urania very much.

Suresh Kotecha was instrumental in introducing me to Vipassana meditation; I am ever indebted.

I had spent two summers of 2008 and 2009, while writing this book, at the Graduate House, University of Toronto. I had a wonderful time with the students to "bounce" some ideas off of; thank you all.

Towards the final days of writing the book, the hospitality of Sanjay and Nimisha Devani, their sons, Sanish and Nishan helped me a lot. Sanjay's mother, Chandaben, shared a lot of wisdom with me. I am ever so grateful for the wonderful time together.

Right in the last days, a solitude at the home of Avnish and Dipti in Montreal sealed the first draft. How could I forget their son and daughter, Rahul and Shalini? I am truly thankful.

Most of all I am grateful to you, the reader. This book exists solely for you. Perchance, should you be inspired by this journey, in your own way, you may help continue it in perpetuity.

Finally, I thank my ego for its persistence to finish the book. I do so respectfully from a safe distance! (How can I justify such a conundrum? Even though ego is very pernicious, mind itself is supple to be tamed, albeit with perseverance and tenacity. It is mind training itself! I leave it to the book to explain the conundrum.)

In the myriad of making of this "offering", if I miss any one, please accept my sincere apology and gratitude.

May all beings be happy!

Note: If you can deeply contemplate as to how any conditioned thing such as making of this book or a pot can happen; kudos to you!

PREFACE

In my teens, I joined scouts so that I could carry a knife. The folding of the scarf and putting it on with a string looped around it mesmerized me. Oh and the medals and beret! It was wonderful. At the camp, we used to play a game, which is engraved in my mind. Two teams were formed. The leading team was given a head start to go as fast as they can but were to make sure to leave a marking, such as an arrow drawn on ground or on a tree trunk when changing direction. Also some "treasures" were buried on the way marked with an X. On the path, these were pointed to by drawing an arrow attached to a square specifying the number of steps to be taken. Once reaching a congenial destination, a big circle was drawn circumscribing an X. All the boys then hid on nearby trees, in the crags, in the hills etc. The second team pestered the scout leader to start the chase immediately, but was allowed only after a decent delay. The duty of the team was to follow the trail, collect the "treasures" and catch all the boys of the first team.

This book has such nuggets strewn along the way. Many a story, that influenced me are woven into a tapestry that gives a picturesque scenery to the journey.

The word "treasure" reminds me of a story I read in my youth.

A king used to watch his citizens going about their ways from a balcony in the early morning before going to court. He pitied a poor man in rags traversing the road at exactly the same time every morning. The king called his vizier to donate a bag full of coins to the old man. The vizier suggested that such a gift might harm him if it is not in his karma. The king agreed. But how could they decide that the gift is or is not in his karma? The vizier suggested that they put the bag in his path the next morning with a couple of soldiers protecting it from others. On that day, it so happened that the poor man, on his way to the market to beg, thought that he might soon lose his eyesight due to aging. Why not practice to walk with eyes closed?

The reader has so many treasures in front of him. But which treasures, if any, are to be had in his/her karma!

DISCLAIMER

I have taken the liberty to expound the rudimentary, scaled down aspects of meditation for the benefit of the reader with the understanding that it CAN NOT replace the technique taught by teachers in a formal setting. The main thrust of my expose is to give a taste of meditation to a novice reader at the initial stage simply because the experience of meditation is of utmost importance in the journey. Without the practice of meditation, the import of subtle insights is lost. Once the technique is understood and the reader is ready to commit, there are many types of meditations to find one that suits his personality. If the reader is already following his own meditation technique, he may continue it with awareness emphasized.

Everyone is unique with a unique journey. Enjoy!

FOREWARD

WHY WRITE SUCH A BOOK?

Every one wants to be happy. It is paramount.

All ads, directly or indirectly, peddle it. There are books written to guide you to acquire it. Even the U.S. Constitution demands that the pursuit of happiness is an unalienable right for its citizens.

It is disappointing, then, to many when such a fundamental goal of happiness is found to be elusive. Happiness cannot be bought nor can it be coaxed by force, pleading or persuasion.

What can one do?

To start one has to ask the right question. What is the cause of unhappiness?

In one's search for an answer to this question one has to fathom the workings of the mind. In doing so one goes to the root of the problem and, understanding its cause, deals with it. Happiness, then, may follow and if not, at least one objectively knows the reasons of his unhappiness. In this way, one finds a solution.

I was looking for reasons of what had I done wrong to suffer a misfortune I thought I did not deserve.

This book is the journal of the journey I undertook in search for an answer. From the depths of despair the journey leads me to the path of Truth. I feel confident that it gives me direction to Reality.

Ego is pernicious. Perhaps I contrive above reasoning with false modesty to enhance my name – an attempt at immortality? At any rate, I do wish to bequeath this book to future generations.

WHY SUCH A TITLE?

The title of the book "A Journey in the 4th Dimension" is to attract readership in modern times. Usually, Time is the fourth dimension, other three being spatial. Towards the end of the book, a "surprising" new set of dimensions is discovered, covering, in essence, the journey from a new perspective.

HOW THE BOOK WAS WRITTEN?

In the Vipassana meditation course, there are theoretical aspects in the discourses that accompanied the practical meditation. I was inspired to read more about the Buddha's teachings. It occurred to me that this is a tremendous opportunity to share my experience, from a personal perspective, of Buddha's teachings, dharma.

The impetus of undertaking the journey hinges upon crucial episodes. These are briefly described here in the spirit of truthfulness. No blame or recrimination is directed to any one. The mere fact that I feel no bitterness or rancor is a testament to the validity of the path. Also, I discovered that I was the one to be blamed.

It is so.

Towards early morn when you are half asleep and half awake, neither here nor there and, ironically, both here and there, you kind of float with the letters of the alphabet making sentences of exquisite beauty. Pearls of words shine in front of you with a chime of bells melodious to your ears. A little change here and some there, you feel attuned to the rhapsody never 'fore experienced. You get up from your reverie and suddenly the mirage of your masterpiece starts to melt rapidly. You desperately try to memorize the text by repeatedly going over the text or feverishly write it down or try to record it. With as much recollection as possible you try to soak up bits of what has just transpired, gratefully salvaging whatever you can.

It is so.

Sometimes the episode occurs when you suddenly wake up in the middle of the night or occasionally, as you are about to fall deep into sleep. No matter how, the lost words are gone forever with a tantalizing after-taste of something exquisite. Yet happy to capture whatever you can, you continue writing.

It is so.

All through the adornment of the writing style as described, contents of the text, though similarly inspired, were coalescing over the previous few days before writing the episode. Then there were many "dry" days when attempts to write became superfluous. Towards the end some loose ends were tied up for readability.

It is so.

In such a way, this book is written, after many months of vacillating, starting in the summer of 2007. It is important to remember that the basic material of the text, in large part, is intuitively experienced at a subjective level as imparted herein.

So it is.

WHAT SHOULD A READER EXPECT FROM THE BOOK?

The book is a practical primer on self-empowerment. It is also an attempt to break the barrier of mundane existence inveighed by routine acceptance of the currency in vogue. As such it breathes in fresh air in one's life by providing, through practical experience, an alternative view. All through life one searches outside of oneself for understanding one's predicament – one's existence. An insight through reflection brings about wonderful results in one's life.

To give an overview of the substance of the book upfront, I present a very condensed, conceptual metaphoric view of the path:

We carry a monkey on each shoulder; one constantly craves and clings while the other detests and abhors every instant depending upon our thoughts (except for rare neutral thoughts). Virtually all our lives, we habitually pander to their needs. Through meditation, we become aware of these monkeys and their antics. Armed with this knowledge, with perseverance and detached observation, we can rid ourselves of them. This gives us empowerment and serenity. This process will be very clearly understood by one following the path.

Finally, this presentation is meant only as a guide to the reader to follow. Never taking it for granted, the reader is to investigate its efficacy and chart his/her own path.

PART ONE
ON THE ROAD...

INTRODUCTION

It is a wonderful life. You are in good health, happily married, children doing well at school, a decent job and caring supportive friends and family members. Annual vacation getaways, regular parties, playing tennis and bridge, reading intellectual magazines and books make up your routine. Cold, flu and kids' growing up pain and tantrums make life challenging but manageable. Regular religious attendance, community service and donations provide spiritual solace. Helpful by nature, you are honest and hardworking. You dispense off social obligations and grudgingly pay your taxes and traffic tickets. A middle class Canadian, you fit admirably in the well-oiled schema of your universe. One day you plan to help the disadvantaged in the society and to help alleviate the poverty in the third world countries. All told it is a wonderful life.

Wait a minute. A long strand of grey hair is growing in my eyebrow. This on my 40th birthday! What is going on? Me? Already?

Suddenly the deaths of family members and friends make you think of your own mortality. Panicked by the uncertainty, you re-double your efforts to protect your family from the vicissitudes of changing circumstances. "Catching up" to the perceived goal of financial security makes you take chances on the stock market. At work, you are not used to politics. As days pass by, you are resigned to let things happen: losing interest and control. Years roll by; a quiet squall before the storm.

Middle age blues depress you; irritation, anger at the slightest provocation and frustrations are the order of the day. You try very hard to make ends meet since acquiring an expensive home for the growing kids. You hope that the investment in the new home will pay off handsomely in your retirement. The stock market crash sets you off tens of thousands of dollars. There is a rumour going on that the company you are working for is downsizing. You suddenly wakeup in the middle of the night, your internals "burning"; you go to the basement so as not to disturb your family. You pace feverishly: mentally wrestling against the uncertainties of your situation. High mortgage payments, uncertain employment future and failed investment in the stocks take their toll on your health.

Your spouse drops a bombshell telling you of that all is not well. She had put up with you and wants to divorce you, now that the children are grown up. That January night, you walk around your neighbourhood without an overcoat, oblivious to the freezing temperature. The brand new buildings look eerie in the soft moonlight while you walk crying. You are laid off from the work that you spent the best years of your life doing! Slowly the friend circle diminishes and relatives are at a distance. Every one you knew really wants to help out but the trammels of every day existence restrict his or her efforts. You are on your own.

Why me? What have I done to deserve this? What could I have done to avert this? What would happen if health fails? What would become of the boys? Your mettle comes off its mooring; your confidence shattered. Mechanically, you go through routines of divorce, of layoff and of selling your home. Downtrodden, with a feeling of utter despair, reality sinks in, in slow motion, in a very painful slow motion -very, very slowly.

Many a times, you contemplated ending your life; the wheels of commuter trains inviting. You even read books at the library to scientifically do it. It was a difficult episode with, thankfully, no guts to carry it out.

All through your slow downfall and grieving, you grasp to make sense of it all, to cope with it. Disbelief, despair, anger, and a gamut of fluctuating and contradictory emotions like guilt and hope run through their course before you accept your reality.

The catastrophe prompts one to investigate how one got into the thick of this, why one living "straight" by the accepted moral principles - or so one believed - was so rejected.

How can one investigate? Where to start?

This is my particular journey to the Truth, an ongoing process of trial and error with human limitations. Yet intuitively I feel that the step taken is in the right direction -intuitively because the process is, by nature, "insightful" defying any conventional concept. The "skeletal" experiences of personal nature in the odyssey are only meant to underpin the concepts in consideration.

This is a journey for anyone, who wishes to experience the Truth, his or her own Truth. How does one make such a journey? At the outset, it is clear that one has to go to the depths of the mind, one's own mind, to analyze its working in a scientific, detached way.

What is the Truth? The investigation penetrates through a layered structure, not unlike an onion, peeling a layer reveals an inner layer at a deeper level.

I hope that the reader is encouraged that making his own trail for the journey is, to say the least, interesting if not rewarding in many ways.

Not to waste reader's time, I have endeavoured to be economical in the delivery of the subject matter. Besides, any elaboration on my part may unduly shade the reader's truth -yet the intricate nature of things has to be conveyed. The reader is empowered to make this distinction. However, concise delivery requires the reader to ponder, meditate and internalize (i.e. experience) on the issues under discussion. The journey by necessity requires reflection, lots of it.

Finally, it must be understood that everyone's journey is unique. The purpose of this document is to empower the individual to choose from available options by developing one's own deep insights. All through life, one mechanically tries to find solutions outside of oneself without realizing the wealth of knowledge within. Also, one may compare notes by reading others' viewpoints but may accept or reject ideas according to one's own inclination and insights.

Certain parts of the text are indented with three different icons for the benefit of the reader:

   Meditation techniques and instruction

   Further explanations, insights, examples, etc.

   My own experience, tests for the reader, helpful ideas, etc.

This way the reader can skip certain indented sections with ease on subsequent reading of the material. In addition, a depiction of "stacked stones" is sometimes placed within the text to allow the reader to reflect on a question before reading further for the answer. As mentioned before, if the reader has been established in a meditation technique, she can omit reading it but it is important to realize that the practice and theory (or insights) go together. Again, it must be understood that the described meditation technique is not a substitute for formal teaching; it is only a "starter" to fast track people to "taste" the sample.

The book may also be treated as a living manual with reader's inputs, ideas, answers to tests, etc. He is encouraged to participate, enabling him to spontaneously be part of the journey, since the experience so charted will be invaluable for his analysis of the Truth. All the reader's inputs are to be entered in an accompanying exercise book or electronic medium with entry of time, date and a reference number (as provided and bolded in parentheses). The inputs and answers provided by the reader are the milestones of his/her journey. The questions are designed to record the progression of the journey.

   Reader is encouraged to state his reason(s) for taking this journey, if possible. He may also write his own life experiences. **(1)**

To set the tone of the journey, let us begin with a delightful cup of tea:

A teacher, upon retiring, went to a Zen master, as was previously agreed, to learn about spirituality. It was customary for a householder to devote more time to contemplate about such matters in the receding years of his life. The Zen master welcomed his friend and invited him to have tea in the garden of the monastery. After an exchange of pleasantries, the master proceeded to pour tea from a pot into a dainty cup, overflowing it. Yet he continued pouring the tea. The highbrowed teacher said with alacrity,

"What are you doing, master san? The tea is overflowing".

"Yes…yes. When the cup is full, it cannot retain any more tea. I see. Same applies to the mind, my dear friend," responded the master.

To prepare for the journey we need the following:

1. Minimal luggage: Emptying the mind so that it is free to suggestions and possibilities, albeit with wise discernment and a healthy discrimination. Enquiry must be encouraged and doubts kept on the back burner to see if they get resolved or dissipated towards the end of the journey. If not, that is our reality.

2. Proper clothing: Protection to ward off the ravages of emotions that may suddenly erupt upon unpleasant revelations. Truth is not necessarily inclined to be benevolent. A hardy thick-skinned attitude to face the reality is necessary to live through these difficulties; and live through them we must with acceptance.

3. A good pair of shoes: Discipline to regularly follow the instructions. Determination is required to give the method a good try. It Matters not that certain aspects are not fully understood in the beginning; with patience and perseverance one succeeds. What was once incomprehensible may make sense.

Do not judge in the beginning, do not judge in the middle and when you judge in the end, be careful lest you judge yourself.

 Let us begin our journey with an exercise to get our bearings. This is done through meditation. Meditation is an indispensable tool. Three simple steps have to be followed:

1. Close your eyes.
2. Assume a comfortable position, though the lotus position with straight spine is recommended.
3. With your mind's eye, follow the passage of the breath in the nostril(s). No attempt should be made to control the breath. Be aware of incoming breath and outgoing breath, right where it touches the nostril(s); it matters not whether it is left or right or both nostrils.

We will do this important exercise for 5 to 10 minutes. Bear in mind that when the mind wanders away, ever so gently, without any guilt or recrimination, bring the attention back to the awareness of breathing

Let us now start. Close your eyes….

 My dear reader, what are your experiences? **(2)**

 Following were the experiences of the meditators:

1. Went to sleep
2. Could not concentrate
3. Fleeting mind with repeated monologue, like needle stuck in a groove of a playing record

4. Could not bring back the attention to breathing
5. Felt peaceful
6. Distracted by surrounding noise
7. Waiting for the time to finish, no experience

Many more experiences could be added to the list.

Phew. What a mind? Could not be controlled even for a second? This is one truth. We experience it.

Such is the state of mind in the world. How could anyone make important life decisions effectively with such a fleeting mind? (Mind is the most important aspect of our existence.) In our search for Truth, we must calm the mind.

A wild horse is trained with discipline, a daily routine of exercising round and round in an enclosed area. A good trainer has a rapport with the horse, a loving tenderness and horse's sense (forgive my pun) of meting out the right dose of exercise. As the training progresses, the trainer is attuned to the idiosyncrasies of the horse. Whoa. With patience and perseverance, (s)he gains the obedience and, more importantly, the friendship of the horse.

Our journey starts with the awareness of the following observations. Mind matters most. We must understand the workings of the mind and use it to our advantage in our search for Truth. Meditation is an important tool in our journey of discovery.

Let us first tease out an important truth to understand the Universe: impermanence.

Chapter 1
IMPERMANENCE

At the beginning of a chapter we will identify the expected understanding of it, a signpost.

Signpost: to get the "feel" of impermanence phenomena and to "intuitively" find the key to carry on our investigation of the Truth.

❦ Since this is the beginning of the journey, it will be a little difficult to follow. The first signpost is also very complex, compounding the difficulty. But once the concept of impermanence is brought into focus, the rest of the journey will be easier, my dear striver.

Parables, imagery, anecdotes and the like are powerful means of communicating abstract or difficult ideas. These are borrowed from diverse well-known sources. We have already used some and continue to do so to spice up our journey.

❦ Siddhartha dove deep in the flowing river and surfaced. He looked around and asked this question to himself,

"Did the river change while I dove?"

The flow of the water suggested that the river had changed. Inquisitively, he then asked,

"Did I change?"

✹   On my birthdays, when I was a child not so long ago, I used to try very hard to stay awake for midnight in the hope to see angels pull me at hands and legs to make me taller, to grow. Sleep, unfortunately, took over my curiosity and when I did manage to keep awake till midnight, I had lost my innocence. Sweet were those days.

Seriously, my dear friend: Do you think Siddhartha changed during his dive? Give reasons. **(3)**

Of course he changed, whether he dove or not.

Everything changes. Nothing remains the same even for an instant.

How did he know this fact two and a half thousand years ago?

🪷   My friend, this is your journey, your experience, your Truth. Don't let Siddhartha or a scientist or I bamboozle you with such antics.

Before we continue, let us meditate.

1. Close your eyes.
2. Assume a comfortable position.
3. Watch your breath at the nostril(s), coming in, going out. Feel the flow of the air.

Do not think of impermanence. Do not think of anything but be aware of the flow of the breath and only the breath for 10 minutes. Let us do it…

 What happened this time? Was it the same as before? **(4)**

Mental constructs are not easy to change. But by perseverance, ever so gently, you will win over your mind. No guilt or recriminations need to be attached. Just do your job.

Let us go back to impermanence.

Intuitively, it does make sense. Does it not? Seasons, plant cycles, rain cycles and life cycles exhibit change. Motions of the planets, suns and galaxies follow a pattern of cycles within a cycle within a cycle. Even within an atom, the pattern continues. Everything moves. So at a microscopic level, it makes sense, as proven by scientific experiments, that there is no rigidity, only flux.

If every thing is in flux, it raises loads of questions.

 What questions do you have, dear reader? **(5)**

Who am I? I have hands and legs to move, mouth to eat food, mind to think, etc. I breathe, I procreate, I reason, I feel, etc. How could I not exist? Is life a dream? Is it a hoax?

It feels like we are falling down (or up?) without a parachute, a free fall.

What do we make of impermanence?

It sure is scary. We, somehow, have to have a handle on this. Let us make some informed choices. If I stand in the middle of the street and a bus runs over me, nothing should happen since the bus and I are not solid; mere vibrations. This of course is not true. To get out this conundrum let us say that there are two realities: absolute and relative. What we discussed is the absolute reality. Relative reality is the stuff of our existence. We experience it daily. Please do not attempt to stand in front of an oncoming bus!

Impermanence, does it make sense?

 Either way let us:

    1. Close our eyes.
    2. Assume a comfortable position, and
    3. Observe our breath…

    Some of us are plainly reading without meditating. The importance of meditation cannot be oversold. It is the sole means of making our mind our friend and, thereby, enables us to find Truth. Please do it!

Let us recap: There is no solidity since everything is in flux. We some how exist with mind, body and consciousness. The best way to understand this is to use the analogy of a candle.

Have a look at a burning candle. The flame melts the wax giving heat and light. The candle gets shorter and shorter. By analogy flame is the consciousness, wax the mind/body aggregate and burning the living. Look closely at the base of the flame. It seems that the flame is replaced by another flame, which in turn is replaced by another one, ad infinitum. You really could not hold on to a particular flame and say that it is a flame. It is in a flux.

 Now look at the electric light bulb when it is on. Does it change?

What do you think Comrade? **(6)**

Of course the light bulb changes. If it did not, why are you paying those electricity bills? In the burning candle scenario, the frequency of "apparent" change was within the spectrum of our eyes' ability to "see" the change while the frequency of the light bulb was too rapid to detect the change. Nothing, but nothing, is constant. Everything is in a flux.

Somehow at a minuscule level, flux congregates to form an apparent material, a body. Still in flux, the aggregation has an instantaneous form and another form appears in the next instant to be followed by another one, akin to the frames of film in a movie. At a fast clip, we get the impression of solidity. Of course, it is more complex than this.

Perhaps you can formulate and reconcile the relative and absolute realities. **(7)**

What do we make of impermanence now?

We made two observations, which are profound: aggregation forms and only for an instant. This means that form requires space and instant requires time. The perception of space and time is inherent in mind/body/conscious phenomena, thereby giving us relative reality. Perhaps understanding the bridge between absolute and relative realities may shed light on our perception of space and time. Look again at the burning candle: the elusive form passes the "torch" from one to the next in an indefinable instant. From a scientific perspective that instant could be attempted to be defined as some fraction of a second.

   What are your thoughts? **(8)**

An instant can never be defined. Suffice it to say that for relative reality, it is required to get over rough edges. Even so, these are conceptions and conceptions are speculations. Bear these in mind as we continue our journey and be ready to discard any notions that defy our intuitive analysis, our Truth.

Who am I? It seems that I am a mind/body aggregate with consciousness. It means our life is continuously going through frame after frame of rising and disappearing at an elemental level. At a gross level, it is perceived to be solid. If so, how does it relate to our daily experience? "I" is just a label for practical purposes in our day-to-day reality. "I" is given a name to identify a coherent "mass of vibrations"; so is "table" for its utility. In relative reality, one tends to take one's "I" as a tangible object. It is ingrained in our psyche, not having the understanding of absolute reality. This is normal. We now know better.

🪷 It is of utmost importance to realize that all through the book any concept such as above is to be "thought through" thoroughly since, as mentioned before, one has to "walk the walk" oneself. Also, such contemplation should not be carried into one's meditation practice, which is absolutely "stand-alone".

Does it mean that we give up everything? Live like a robot till we die? Or live your life without any regard for anyone or anything? This is a nihilistic view.

 What do you think, buddy? **(9)**

Of course not, not at all! Out of nothing, we are made of nothingness. What a miracle? This is a time for celebration. Roll the drums, blow the trumpets, dance and be merry. Intuitively, it seems that we have a purpose in life. Rather than speculate about it, enjoy the ride for the journey itself may be its purpose. At any rate, being aware of our ignorance of absolute reality liberates us from many mundane problems in our existence. This gives us an impetus to enjoy being human.

🪷 Life is a precious gift; do not waste it. Utilize it to its maximum potential. While we search for the truth, let us not be glum. Be human. Enjoy. With this insight, our search will continue to unravel other truths.

The congregation of aggregates (vibrations) repeatedly formed "you" (cycles of vibrations) and your life (a bigger cycle).

If everything is in a flux, is there anything to hold on to?

🪷 Siddhartha, contemplating the nature of things as fluid and in constant flux, looked for something to hold on to, something to grasp in the morass of a whirling Universe. There was nothing that "truly" existed. For his experiment, he needed something for reference; as a scientist needs a time-piece or a navigator a compass. To a meditator, breath is an anchor from which to observe life's flow throughout one's lifetime. Breath will do.

Breath is with us all through our lives. It is the rhythm of living.

You may get the inkling of the significance of breath as you progress on your journey.

For now, when we observe the breath, we are trying to pinpoint our attention to a very precise space at any instant and the instant after, etc. We are in fact watching our own living akin to the burning of the candle analogy discussed previously, albeit at a higher frequency.

Mon ami, we have a long way to go.

🧘 Meditation is our ticket to our salvation or at least to make informed, judicious choices in real life. Let us firm up our meditation technique:

1. Close our eyes.
2. Assume a comfortable position, and
3. Observe the passage of the breath touching the nostril(s). Without any association, observe the breath, its heaviness or lightness, its temperature or any observation about the breath. We shall do it for 15 to 20 minutes. Remember to bring back the wandering mind to the breath without any guilt or recriminations.

Let us start....

  What is your experience? **(10)**

Even if you cannot observe your breath for a second during the whole session, do not worry. Maybe next time, you may do better. But do not give it a second thought!

Meditation is so simple that it is difficult to do. Actually there is nothing to do. It would be easier if you do not think about it; just ease into that empty state. Relax. Let it be. Less said the better.

We have answered some of the questions about impermanence. Through meditation, we have tried to calm our mind and we will continue to do so. Intuitively we have a weak grasp on relative and absolute realities. As we continue we will feel more confident about our discoveries.

Dear friend, look at the posted signpost at the beginning of this chapter. Have you got a feel for impermanence? Do you feel that meditation holds the key to continue our search for Truth?

You are free to change the signpost according to your liking.

  Write your comments, observations, etc. **(11)**

  Recap your take on impermanence: Write it, please. **(12)**

You may well ask, "What has all this philosophizing got to do with my problems?" Patience, dear friend, is a virtue. Understanding impermanence at its root level will help us in a practical way. I believe that difficult concepts should be dealt with early on to ponder upon in our journey.

Chapter 2
LESSONS OF IMPERMANENCE

Signpost: Get a better grip on the impermanence phenomena. Use the experience of impermanence in daily life to our advantage. Solidify our meditation.

The last chapter was difficult to comprehend. It is important to understand the reality of impermanence at its root level. But even if we do not understand it in detail, but have a "feel" for it, we are ready to continue.

Before we continue let us recap: At a very elemental level, every thing is in flux. There is no solidity. There are two realities, absolute and relative (or apparent). We had attempted to analyze absolute reality with limited success. Our aim here is to focus in relative reality with the understanding that meditation holds the key in our search for Truth.

At this juncture, a new element is introduced in our journey. Allocate about a 1 to 2 hour period once in the coming next few days to "waste" on the following: weather and conditions permitting, watch clouds move in the sky or watch the falling of snow. The methodology of concentrated observation, as it was done for watching the breath in meditation, is to be applied in this experiment. This should be done from a comfortable place without any distractions. We shall touch base on this later.

Let us tackle impermanence in our every day existence.

☸ The first time I became aware of death was when I was 16 years old. My father's body was brought home from the hospital for embalming/preparation before carrying it for cremation. All the family members were crying, grieving, trying to comfort each other. There was an eerie feeling of suspended-ness and numbness. Time hung heavy. We children were allowed to see him quickly and then returned protectively to other rooms. In that brief moment, it was unnerving to see my father in a deep sleep, never, as I surmised from others, to be back.

My dear fellow traveler, what is your take on the subject of death? **(13)**

Death raises profound questions about life and the feeling of loss lasts for some time. Then time heals. Life continues. The feeling of impermanence, so graphic and profound, slowly attenuates to a low level.

Before we continue our meditation, let us revisit the basis of our meditation in detail so that there is no doubt about the technique and its efficacy in our journey.

The technique is simply to observe the breath, coming in and going out, with our mind's eye; keeping eyes closed (not to be distracted) and having a comfortable position (not to be distracted, again). It is important to understand that none of our discussions interfere with meditation; for that matter nothing else should. There should not be any feeling of failure or success; guilt or euphoria, expectation or recrimination, joy or sorrow. Simply practice like playing scales on a piano. If the mind wanders, observe its escapades and the moment you realize that it has, gently bring it back to the awareness of the touching of the breath in the nostril(s). Simply become aware of if it is fast or slow; hot or cold; heavy or light without giving any importance to it. If you become adept at not giving any label to these feelings (that is to analyze that label of "hot" is the opposite of "cold"), so much the better. Just observe, observe, observe.

By meditating so, you are bringing your attention to the reality of the present moment. The mind is arrested; its chatter brought to a halt even for a moment.

For thousands of years, peoples of all persuasions and ilk, everywhere in the world, have experienced that meditation has opened the "gates" of their understanding of the Universe. You, my dear colleague, shall not blindly follow any one but experience your own truth. Meditation is your ticket, your own ticket. However, you may take advice from or compare your notes with the ones who have treaded this path. This will expedite your journey without compromising your independent "experience".

Let us meditate for 20 minutes.

On the fourth day of a 10 day retreat at a meditation course, I had an "out of body" experience. I was looking down on the Earth, way above the clouds, floating like an astronaut. It happened suddenly and took me by surprise. The moment I realized what was happening, the "bubble" burst and I was back. I thought I had achieved nirvana; no need to continue the course. At lunchtime, I booked an appointment with my teacher fully expecting to be given instructions to refine and finalize my technique, and let go.

The teacher and a manager listened to my experience. The manager let out a muffled chuckle and then pretended to clear her throat.

"Chandu, please pay attention to the breath…" the teacher said.

"But I was out of…." I tried to protest.

"… at the nostrils. You have a colourful imagination."

What is life? What is its meaning?

 What are your thoughts, my dear comrade? **(14)**

These esoteric questions lead to speculation, and thereby to conceptions. Conceptions are extraneous baggage, which hinder our journey. Travel light, my colleague. If persistent, keep these issues on the back burner for a while. On the path, you may deal with these questions in your own way.

🪷 However, certain concepts, like our understanding of impermanence, the two realities, etc., are necessary and are to be later discarded akin to a canoe to be abandoned once across the river.

Perhaps the meaning of life will be apparent, in our own terms, as we deduce how to live it!

☸ How do you play your hand of impermanence, my dear gambler? **(15)**

We already touched upon "I", a label given to an ever changing yet seemingly solid entity. It is futile to hold on to such a label. Not understanding this, a mindset of ego develops to convince oneself of solidity and one's own separate existence. It continues to "protect" one not unlike a very concerned mother. To thwart the lurking dangers, it continually improves its techniques of convincing one to do its bidding. After gaining ground, it controls through pampering, coaxing, threatening or whatever means it takes to protect "itself", for it has acquired a persona. Ego is not conducive to live properly. It gives its owner a false sense of importance. At worst, it blocks openness to new ideas necessary to experience life fully. It is a huge baggage. When detected in fellow travellers, do not share it, but ignore it. In our journey, we recognize it and try to minimize its impact.

A Bedouin was snugly sleeping in his tent on a cold night under the canopy of a glittering star-laden sky. His camel stuck his head in the tent and said,

"Master, it is freezing cold. May I at least keep my head in the tent to keep warm?"

"Sure, you may"

After a while the forefeet, torso and the tail were accommodated with difficulty in the small tent. Once in, the camel felt a bit cramped. He booted the Bedouin out!

The camel has usurped the tent.

Do not confuse ego with a zest to live. Life, a precious jewel, has to be preserved and enjoyed.

The second lesson of impermanence is ownership; "mine" is a corollary to "I". How can anything belong to you when even your life does not? It is another big baggage. Do not give away your things yet! Remember life is a beautiful gift to be enjoyed. Knowing reality you make judicious choices, keep (essentials) or discard, spend or economize, give (donations) or take (dues). If blessed with wealth, do not squander. If you are poor, strive to earn your keep. If endowed with wisdom, do not boast; if not, endeavour to acquire it. Life is a learning process. Enjoy making decisions. If you make mistakes, so be it. Enjoy what you have because you may lose it.

Another lesson of impermanence is detachment. Since nothing lasts forever, there is no need to "grasp" or to "perform". Your life is simplified. Guilt, anger, passion, frustrations are controlled. You face the vicissitudes of life with equanimity. Pain will not last forever, nor does ecstasy. Practically, you have already started the process of equanimity in meditation. Without attaching any importance to the outcome of meditation, you have been aware of your breath moment to moment. Again, you also did not give any brook to the wanderings of the mind. In daily life, this lesson teaches us to deal with life's ups and downs with resolve and rectitude, with a healthy attitude towards the outcome.

Let not detachment lull you into inaction. To enjoy life, you have to be active, with alacrity and vigour, a sense of purpose and confidence. Live!

If a lion were to chase you, run. For heaven's sake run like you never did before. This is not the time to think about impermanence or detachment or any abstract philosophy.

If a woman is molested in the middle of the night in an alley on your way home, fight with all your ability. This is your duty as a citizen and a fellow voyager.

Yet another lesson of impermanence is awareness of the present moment. Past is but history and future is not even borne. By concentrating on the present moment, we can resolve problems requiring deep insights, efficiently. Also we live life to the fullest extent; enjoy that flavoured ice cream neither reminiscing (past) about it nor desiring (future) it. Again, this we have practiced in meditation: awareness of breaths from moment to moment.

You will be surprised how you enjoy life more and more as time goes by. Many aspects of life resolve easily, automatically.

Makes you go for meditation right now, doesn't it? Let us do it.

All the above ideas require a lot of reflection, as mentioned at the start of our journey. Reader has a lot to ponder about. It is helpful to realize that with the practice of meditation, some of these insights crop up automatically with clarity and ease. These insights may stubbornly happen in our meditation, but, ever so gently, upon realizing their occurrence, do firmly observe breath and only breath and nothing but breath.

What else does impermanence teach us, my compatriot? **(16)**

How about death? It surely teaches us how to live. Live well. Enjoy. You never know when your time is up.

What happens at death? Let us go to the analogy of the burning candle. Suppose towards the end of a candle, we light another one with the dying (pun) flames of the present one. The flame (consciousness) is transferred to the next candle (mind/

body aggregate), another life (energy). Remember this is only an analogy.

Did I bamboozle you again with my antics? Do not accept any ideas like a meek sheep. Do not be naive. Be brave like a lion. Question my analyses. Ponder on the subject matter: impermanence, death.

What do you think? Roar. Make your mark, my dear hunter. **(17)**

Did we reach our signpost? Please analyze and make your comments. **(18)**

When impermanence is observed in our daily lives, it gives us impetus to strive for Truth. We also turn its understanding to live our short life "fully". As we continue to meditate, we become more and more aware of these things automatically.

Chapter 3
5-STAR HOTEL

You have worked very hard; travelled a very strenuous path. You deserve a rest. This is important. There is no need for a signpost at a hotel.

Did you get a chance to reflect on moving clouds or falling snow?

Did your reflection make you ponder about impermanence? Meditation? Life?

My dear, dear voyager! You fell into a trap! I saved you from being run over by a bus, eaten by a lion and now I have to extricate you from a very common trap.

Tch! Tch!

All reflections are to be done fully absorbed in the activity itself, moving of clouds or falling of snow. In watching the clouds, for instance, see the colour of the sky, the shape and whiteness of the clouds, their speed, and their size. These are to be done without any ownership of the process of doing it. Immersed within, you feel the adjectives, no more, no less.

Did you discern a cloud to be cumulus or cirrus? You fell in back in the trap again! Did you notice your ego trying to show off your knowledge about clouds?

Repeat this exercise while you are at this magnificent hotel. This way you will take the needed rest after a difficult journey. Empty your mind of concepts, ideas, anything at all. Plainly observe the natural activity of cloud or snow. Relax!

 How do you feel? **(19)**

 Next let us do the meditation for half an hour.

Refreshed?

This is a good time, after being refreshed to catch up on our experience of the journey so far, in the luxury of the hotel before we continue. An extra day will do us good. We deserve it.

 What are your experiences? **(20)**

To reiterate: Life itself is a journey. It is full of ups and downs, always changing. To get the best of life, we have to concentrate on living in the moment, the sum of which will give us the insight to do the right thing: get rid off extraneous baggage, enjoy being human and live peacefully.

How do we measure our progress? Are we headed in the right direction?

Let us conceptually go to the beginning of our journey. How were you affected by what happened to you? Anger, guilt, jealousy, hatred or any such feeling consumed you. As such you felt burning inside, depressed, green with envy, intense dislike, etc. These "ate" your innards, disturbed your sleep and affected your day-to-day activities. If there is even a slight reduction in the intensity of these negative feelings, my good fellow, we made progress. As for direction, what better indication then that you feel better and more peaceful!

Meditation, inherently, is a key to unlock the understanding of our Universe, our own Truth.

We are ready to move on with a spring in our step and confidence in our search.

Chapter 4
LES MISÉRABLES

(I am listening to Lucciano Pavoratti on the radio as I write this piece; a fantastic life!)

Signpost: a glimpse at the causes of suffering in our lives.

Take any newspaper today and scrutinize the front page. Of all the articles mentioned, see how many are dealing with tragedies, deaths, disasters, etc., in the world; some close to home. Television news reinforces these tragedies with vivid images.

It is a fact that in life one has to go through birth, aging, illness, ups and downs of living, and death. Let us not forget the joy of living, the effort of overcoming the difficulties, and the opportunities afforded to make our mark. Above all, celebrate the gift of life!

It seems that unwanted things happen while desired things do not. While some undeserving person wallows in riches, you are mired in poverty despite honest hard work.

 What doest thou think, oh seeker of Truth? **(21)**

There is suffering in life. We will analyze the cause(s) of our misfortunes objectively, so that we may be prepared to deal with them, if not eradicate them.

It is time for meditation. This time we shall introduce one more aspect of the meditation technique. While watching with the mind's eye the breath at the nostril(s), we are also aware of any sensations that crop up in the area under the nose and above the lips. When we feel tingling, scratching, piercing, warmth, coldness or any other sensation in that area we divert our attention there. We simply observe the phenomena detachedly; see how long it lasts for the law of impermanence dictates that any thing that arises will disappear. After observing its passing, simply bring the awareness back to the breath at the nostril(s), watching again for any other sensation that may crop up in the prescribed area. Be very alert for sensations.

We shall do the meditation for at least 30 minutes.

Write your experience of your meditation. **(22)**

Before we continue our investigation, here is another exercise to be done once in the next few days. Take any activity, such as cooking, gardening or house cleaning. In cooking, for example, clear the kitchen table. Cut each type of vegetable in the recipe and put into bowls separately on the table. Similarly, measure meticulously and place herbs, spices and any other ingredients in different sized bowls. All the preparations must be done with full attention to the process required. Cutting celery, for example, requires washing, peeling skin, and cutting into slices. Each sub-process is to be carried out with the minutest attention. Similarly, the cooking process and clearing of the table are also carried out with utmost concentration. It may be helpful to assume a comfortable, relaxed standing position to do the cutting, for example. No distractions or thoughts should be entertained throughout the cooking. If you did choose cooking it may be a good idea to invite some friends and family. We shall touch base on this later on.

Mind gets its fodder from any of the five senses and the thought process itself. These are its total inputs. When an image strikes the retina, a bundle of nerves carries the image to the brain, where it is processed. A quick check is done to recall a similar image in the memory. If so, reinforce the assessment whether the image was pleasant or distasteful, its intensity dependent upon its repetitions and mental assessment. Sensations of good or bad feeling are felt throughout the body in proportion to the intensity. In turn, reaction manifests. Activation, assessment, sensations and reaction are the main processes carried out at every stimulus from any sense organ or by thought itself.

⚘ Siddhartha analyzed the mental processes that make us behave the way we do in every day life (he actually analyzed the whole chain of processes of birth, life, death and beyond; nature of the mind being within the life cycle). He realized that the assessment by the mind tends to crave pleasant or to detest unpleasant feelings.

The repeated buildup of such feelings leads to a strong desire. Over a period of time the mind is conditioned to pander to the desire reactively; it has resigned. The craving for desire is a cumulative process carried out without our full awareness. It drives the mind. The reasoning process of the mind is "hijacked" into thinking that all is well since how can you, such a logical person ever make a bad decision: manipulation from the ego. Even if you were to come to realize that desire is a bad thing, the ego will don the orange robes with you in full agreement (you will be surprised with his ardor!) and upon gaining your confidence will plant the seeds of doubt; the trick of repetitions is foisted upon you again. It is not the mind per se but the embedded raw desire. It knows the human tendency of taking the easiest route and not to be bothered. In a nutshell, desire is the cause of misery since it pollutes the mind and corrupts its thinking.

The intent behind any action is of utmost importance since desire to achieve wholesome goals in life or to pursue activities such as compassion is commendable. Volition of the thought dictates the fruit of the action. Of course, the definition of desire in the above paragraph is to be taken in this light.

☸ This is a very concise treatise on the subject of desire. I challenge you, my dearest warrior in search of Truth, to tread with utmost care and reflection. Enter your comments please. **(23)**

🧘 This is a good time to meditate. Remember to blank your mind of any analytical thinking. Even if you were to get a mere moment, without distraction, to observe the breath in half an hour, you have done well. Even if not, you have done well. Watch the sensations and their durations without any reactions (no scratching, for example). Let us do it.

Siddhartha looked at the whole cycle of chain reactions and realized that to break the chain we must attack its weakest link: sensations.

In life we cannot stop inputs to the mind. The process of assessment is also spontaneous. The sensations generated by assessment generally go below the radar of our awareness. We feel them as "goose pimples" or "burning" when they have built up; but, consciously again, we do not pay attention but follow through to reaction automatically.

Actually there is no subconscious mind as such. Mind is always conscious, even in deep sleep. A mosquito bite in the middle of the night will induce one to strike out in reaction.

If we are to be aware of the sensations, we have to bring them to be registered by the mind. We then can observe their significance and instead of reacting blindly to the stimulus, we act accordingly.

This is why the awareness of sensations is introduced in our meditation. A small prescribed area for observation is chosen because the smaller the area, the sharper the mind. The more concentrated our awareness to observe the sensation's arising and dissipating, the deeper is our experience of impermanence, an aspect of reality.

But how does this relate to desire and what can we do? Go for it, samurai. **(24)**

Surely sensations are the manifestations of desire, wanting pleasant things to happen and unpleasant things not to happen. There is in no end to the wants of desire, a bottomless pit. In imagination, the artist Desire has painted a beautiful picture of a girl, has sculptured a vivacious figure, dancing romantically a siren dripped in honeyed voice. Woe is the admirer! He is drawn helplessly into this creation, which in reality does not exist.

A battle plan is drawn for you, my dear Alexander. You came, you saw but can you conquer? Your analysis **(25)**

Once the sensations are brought on to the radar screen of awareness, we simply observe their theatrics, detachedly. From the comfort of distance, the unfolding spectacle is observed like a movie, the arising and disappearing of the events. Now the impact of desire gets weaker and weaker as you observe as a spectator. But how about enjoying the company of the girl? Why not? If only you live "reality" in a proper perspective. This time, though, you are in control. You enjoy the moment in reality and not abstractly; you build neither "castles" (past) nor "dreams" (future). Enjoy being human albeit within the constraints of moral precepts (more on this later).

⚘ A student accompanied a renowned Zen master in his travels to villages. Once at a torrent river, the master offered a frightened young girl to carry her across. Upon reaching the other side, the grateful girl parted company and the student and the master continued their journey. That night as they prepared to sleep at an inn the student, a novice, could not help but blurt out,

"How can you carry a beautiful girl across the river, when you profess to have renounced the earthly pleasures, master san?"

"Are you still carrying her in your mind?" replied the master.

Following are composite scenarios of life:

A middle-class Canadian is frustrated in life. First year at work as a lawyer, he already feels the pressures of doing things against his "grain". He is told, in "real" life that is how the cookie crumbles. Accumulated dissatisfaction prompts him to a spiritual search. He puts his efforts in revitalizing his own faith. Disappointed, in desperation, he is attracted to the allure of eastern wisdom. He reads a lot about different 'ism's, attends lectures about them, and practices yoga, tai chi, meditation, etc. Upon hearing of an acclaimed, yet reclusive, yogi, he embarks on a journey to the foothills of the Himalayas. Upon arriving in India, cultural shock, abject poverty and dirtiness almost makes him take the first available flight back to Canada. Thrown in the "soup" of humanity, first time in his life, he feels the connectedness of all things. Dogs, cows, even camels and donkeys share the road with all sorts of people of different culture, religion, caste, dress and language. To a "sanitized" Canadian, brought up in a protected environment, this is a raw experience of living.

Slowly, but surely, after a bout of diarrhea, reality of existence sinks in. Acclimatized, with determination, he travels the arduous journey by train, bus, bullock cart and walking; he reaches his destination only to be told that the yogi has left without a forwarding address. Having been robbed of passport and money, he begs and borrows his way to New Delhi. After acquiring a new passport and infusion of wired money, he is told of a "great soul" in a nearby village. After a ceremony of bhajjans (religious songs) and a lecture on the evils of materialism, he is promptly initiated in the order. It is imperative to part with worldly belongings. It makes sense, thus, to donate to the order to continue their good work. After skillfully extricating himself, he makes it back to New Delhi, unscathed. Inured by experiences, armed with knowledge of deduction from his professional training and by sheer luck of coming in contact with "right" people, he discovers the path of his choice.

A successful Canadian businessman was looking forward to enjoy his retirement after sacrificing so much time and energy in acquiring wealth. Divorced, now living with a beautiful younger woman, he sold his garment factory since his son was adamant in pursuing a career in graphic design with no interest in business. As a matter of fact his son seemed bent on going against the things he stood for, almost to the point of sadistic revenge of sorts. Refusing help, as was his wont, his son lived in a bachelor apartment, eking out a living. Relations were sour after divorce and his new love. Then the rug was pulled from under his feet: he was diagnosed with lung cancer. Before long his prognosis was that the cancer had metastasized; he had at most six months to live. I met him at this juncture in my volunteering. It did not help that I was of his age bracket. Still, after a few meetings, we became friends. I became his confidante. Fate had dealt a cruel blow. He would not even flinch for a second to give all his wealth for good health, even for less time than his current "life sentence". Looking back, he could easily have lived a comfortable, enjoyable life and not worked so hard. What a waste! The ravages of cancer emaciated him; a lean fragile figure with large eyes. He felt betrayed by the promises of his faith and angrily refused to call in a priest. Towards the end he hallucinated, seeing people behind us, visitors. He would slowly lift his bony finger, staring past us at the corner of the ceiling and say, "Dad...Mum..." in a feeble voice.

On my way back to the shop after a siesta on a hot summer day, I was mildly surprised in seeing a woman in a wheel chair and a young man having beer under the shade of a tree. At the shop, half an hour later, they came in and looked leisurely at toys, kitchen items, rugs and carpets, cosmetics, tools and curios. The woman fondled each item of interest with care and talked in whispers to the man. Now and then there was muffled laughter. After spending about two hours of shopping, they came to the cash register with a few items to purchase. Upon chatting, I realized that the woman had some rare condition, paralyzing her waist down at a very early age and the young man volunteered once a week to take her out for half a day. This time was the highlight to her otherwise confined, prison-like existence. For variety, they had taken two buses to come to this shopping plaza.

At another time, again in the afternoon on a hot summer day, a young woman took two carts of shopping and went through the shop, looking at items seriously. She criss-crossed the shop exchanging items, not quite sure of her decision. Deeply engrossed in her activity, she seemed oblivious to her surroundings. At some length, she came to the cash register with both carts full. Never had I seen a person buy so much in one go. Eager to win over her clientele, I remarked that she might return any item within a week if she brings her receipt. She responded with sadness, "I am a compulsive buyer. I just buried my brother. I would like to kill the drug dealers who took his life."

Never in my life did I feel such a powerful heart-wrenching tug.

⊛ Read the signpost and write your thoughts about it, my dear Viking. **(26)**

Chapter 5
4-STAR HOTEL

When we look back from our vantage point we see that we have covered lots of ground, two steamy mountains with distinct peaks and a glimpse of the path we had traversed. The scene is romantic with an eerie feeling of déjà vu.

The hotel is the best we can get in this remote place. We need to soak our weary limbs and take a good rest. Rest is at least as important as our travels in our journey if not more.

How did your meal turn out? Did the guests like it? Did they comment that you are in the wrong profession? Made you feel warm all over the body, did it not? How did you react to it? Hopefully, with full attention to your sensations, warm feeling in the stomach and thumping of blood in the heart. Even if you did not, but somehow felt the ego pumping you up, you did very well. Practice makes one perfect, so goes the adage.

The whole process of cooking required your full attention at every step. Every moment was to be fully lived. This was the most important aspect of the process -mindfulness.

We shall get up early in the morning and go for a little walk for about an hour in this beautiful setting. With a glimpse, now and then, of the scenery, we shall actually concentrate on walking; at every step we will endeavour to feel the sensation of touching the ground, the measured jaunt of each step and the feel of our muscles stretching and contracting. We will also pay full attention to minutest detail of the terrain, the branches to avoid, water puddles to be jumped over. Make sure that our footing is solid and feel the sensations in the sole touching the ground. Fully aware mindfulness!!!

Was it a very attentive and mindful walk? Do you feel refreshed?

It is time for breakfast. We are hungry. A good warrior fills his stomach to about three-quarters full so as to keep alert for the day. Again we have to be aware of eating each morsel, the feel of it in the mouth, the chewing, and the taste of it. Every moment is savoured to its fullest in eating this delicious breakfast. The motions of the hand reaching out for a drink and bringing it to the lips are fully acknowledged. Without talking or looking around we do justice to our repast. Well done!

All the above exercises and also watching clouds, rain or snow and cooking a meal are in the course Mindfulness 101.

Now that we are well fed and refreshed it is time to go to a quiet place to meditate. Since we have eaten recently, we take our time to look around and seep in the surrounding scenery, admiring it with a calm mind. Then slowly we close our eyes….

 How do you feel? **(27)**

It is a good time to reflect upon our journey and refresh our understanding of it.

 This time with a lot of reflections, please write down all your thoughts about our endeavour. This is your journey, your Truth. Be honest and take your time. A good hotel like this deserves your patronage. Enjoy! You deserve the best. **(28)**

We have come to a crossroad of sorts. We must take stock before we continue. How do we know that we have progressed? Are we headed in the right direction? We asked these questions before and had some inkling about their answers. Let us firm up.

A good yardstick to measure progress in our journey is to measure our gratitude in living our lives. Do you feel grateful for things coming your way? Are you appreciative of people doing things for you? Saying "thank you" is widely depreciated in its meaning by mechanically meting it out indiscriminately. Truly measured appreciation is a gem. It comes from within you.

A young girl serving in an airport café was crushed by the orders but smilingly continued. I watched her while sipping coffee from one of the overcrowded tables and saw customers lined up in a throng, some swearing and some going through the motions of getting their coffee with a curt "thank you". I managed to go the coffee machine and when she came to it, said,

"I have been watching you. You are doing a great job. Thank you very much".

She smiled, "No one has told me that before".

Neither had I spontaneously felt grateful before.

When the feeling of gratitude manifests in day-to-day life, it is a sign of progress in your journey. A sense of satisfaction accompanies it. As mentioned before, anger, frustrations and such negative feelings are reduced in their intensity and duration. Positive feelings such as compassion and love manifest automatically. Happy and peaceful by nature, people comment that you are easy to get along with. People who knew you before may show surprise at your transformation.

The anger you felt at the beginning of the journey not only diminished but you felt, in retrospect, that it was futile. You were reacting and it was natural to live through it, initially as your character "makeup" and later as a part of grieving. You now accept your responsibility, at least partially (bravo!), for the problems that developed. You were stubborn in dealing with people, arrogant in your views and of miserable disposition. Your conceited "know it all" attitude at a party was atrocious. You accept reality easily now (so you got a traffic ticket!) and are ready to forgive and forget.

Deep down inside, you feel that the direction of your journey is right.

 Do you? Give your own reasons. **(29)**

What did we learn so far?

There are two realities. Absolute reality dictates impermanence; i.e. everything is in flux and there is no solidity. Relative reality is what we normally experience; apparent solidity with an oblique understanding of impermanence manifested by death, changing of the seasons, landscapes, circumstances, etc.

Life is a continuum flux of consciousness in a mind/body construct. Mind is a repertoire of memory among other things such as comprehension, decision-making, etc. It is also essential to make sense of living. Senses and ideas are its fodder. Any input triggers evaluation by the mind, resulting in sensations in the body and reaction by the person to the stimuli. A constant impingement of evaluation of liking or disliking, craving or hatred for the sense-objects develops. Thus desire consumes one, stoked by the ego, and ruins one's life by its infinite demands; bigger and better forever. Impermanence teaches that there is no need to grasp for anything since nothing lasts forever including our dear life. But desire, embedded in the mind by repetitive demands and in collusion with the ego, makes us believe otherwise. To get rid of it we have to analyze it. To analyze it we have to bring its manifestation - sensations - to our attention. Once we simply observe sensations without attaching any importance to them, the desire diminishes. Thus an adept meditator, while enjoying the sense-objects and being fully aware of sensations, keeps the mind calm. Delusion is thwarted.

In meditation, we simply observe our breath, going in or coming out, where it touches the nostril(s). We also keep an eye on the area below the nostrils and above the lips for any sensations (itching, scratchy, tingling, warm, cold, etc). If a sensation manifests, we simply observe it. Keeping in mind that nothing lasts forever, in meditation we observe sensations with awareness and equanimity, two most important aspects. Awareness keeps our eyes on the ball and equanimity makes us detached, with the understanding of impermanence. Both are requisites to meditate properly.

While meditating, keep the spine straight; this will help in the long run. If you feel uncomfortable during the sitting, you may change the position for a little while and come back to the normal position. Be careful that the mind may want you to keep changing the position by remonstrating, exaggerating the pain, etc. You have to show your mettle; you are the boss. Sometimes your mind is too agitated to meditate. You may walk a little and try to resume meditation; keeping in mind the antics played by the mind. Mind is tricky. With perseverance and patience, and without guilt or recrimination, you deal with the situation. You will see that as time goes by, you will feel less pain and look forward to meditating. You will feel more confident in this as multifarious benefits accrue.

We will meditate for 30 minutes or more…

I have persuaded the owner of the hotel to let us stay one more day at a discounted rate. What do you say, partner?

From atop a secluded hidden crevice, we overlook a lake glimmering in the sun's slanting rays. Such a sight soothes our weary senses. This is a time fully allocated to imbibing nature at its best. No more philosophizing, no more meditation either; just letting ourselves be in the folds of Mother Nature. Life is beautiful and the moment is precious. Enjoy!

At this point in our journey, we have come to realize a very important facet of our endeavour. We meditated with awareness and equanimity and we were mindful in our activities. Awareness, equanimity and mindfulness are meant to arrest our mind to the present moment in rest. Neither contrived nor expectant, we experienced profound stillness and emphatic joy. In the same vein there is one more component realized by Zen Buddhists: "beginner's mind". Remember the cup of tea we shared at the start of the journey? That story emphasizes "emptying" the mind and starting afresh. It is a good idea to forget what we learned so far and go back to the start of our journey and learn for the first time, again. Let us do it. Next few days we are to be reading, meditating, writing notes and experiencing till we reach here to continue forward.

Like a good samurai practicing Zen, we empty our minds and go back to the beginning of the journey - for the first time, again!

How do we know, when we reach here, that it is the second time if we sincerely emptied our mind? We fill the blank in the following famous quote and date it!

"_____ was here (date:__/__/____)"

NOW GO BACK

The purpose of going back was to experience "beginner's mind": to develop a child's curiosity of the world around you with an intention of opening yourself up to ideas you may have missed in the first instance. Compare notes to see if it has. The repetition also reinforces the practice of meditation afresh.

Your Honour, I am guilty as charged. I confess, I lied to you a little or rather I am guilty of negligence in accurate reporting. At the start of the meditation techniques you were told that your mind was weak and fleeting like a monkey. You may have been under the impression that your meditation had been somehow compromised. In my defense, you were, in all fairness, told that it matters not if you succeeded in stilling your mind or not. To set the record straight you actually succeeded simply because you observed the working of your mind! Isn't that fantastic!

Come to think of it, I actually realized this fact recently. As a true historian, I refuse to update my previous take on reality since it gives me the progression of the journey. As a bonus it also gives depth to my reportage. As such, Your Honour, I revise my previous acceptance of guilt to "not guilty, sir".

Ego works in mysterious ways!

With this fresh insight, understand that, no matter whatever happens, the mind has to "ease" into meditation mode, not unlike dandelion pollen floating in air, waiting to settle. Let it be, let it be. Just let it be.

Siddhartha was emaciated, almost on the verge of death, with his tapas as practiced by the strivers of the yore to kill the ego and thereby achieve enlightenment. He was getting nowhere with his search for the cause of misery inflicted upon humanity. He remembered that as a child, he, sitting under a rose-apple tree on a hot summer afternoon, had eased into a trance of indescribable clarity of thought. Why not let the mind slip into its own fold without exerting any effort?

We shall continue our journey with a little change in our format and presentation.

We shall regularly meditate for an hour every day. Select our own time to do it; morning or evening is preferable. We will select a comfortable place to do it. Regular sitting will help us tremendously in our journey.

Since meditation techniques have been thoroughly explained and its schedule established, we should take out writing about it moving forward. But before we do, let me challenge you with the example of "mosquito meditation" to test your understanding of the technique:

As you get comfortable in your regular stance watching your breath touching your nostril(s), you realize that you have company. A mosquito is hovering near your right ear with a monotonous drone. Irritating! Your right hand itches to take action. You curb your violent instincts and direct your attention to locating its position. You become aware of it landing on your right nape, a perfect place to zap it. You feel its proboscis piercing your skin. Ouch! Yet you bless it with love as it flies away. May all sentient beings be happy!

You are a model student with a keen sense of awareness coupled with equanimity. Your compassion and loving kindness ooze out. You get 9 out of 10. Why didn't you get a perfect score? See the next page for the answer!

In the meditation technique that we practice, we put our attention in the area below the nostrils and above the upper lip. Ideally, you should get 0 or 1 out of 10, since you went out of bounds!

Just kidding! the example is a blueprint to aspire to. Remember -we must continue meditating because it is the backbone of our journey, our truth. Without it all is lost.

Chapter 6
JOIE DE VIVRE

We have come a long way. In appreciation of your tenacity, I would like to give you a gift; a gift unmatched in this world; a gift precious as the very life itself. In return all I ask is that you preserve it and share it. The more you use it the more it grows. When you share it, it enhances in its luster and value. That gift is meditation. You already have it.

Signpost: Life is to be lived to the fullest, understanding the nature of action and its effect -karma and karmaphal.

After an arduous journey of understanding impermanence, reality, desire, etc., we come to a path of living life itself!

Before we continue, it is important to once again examine life's "becoming" – a driving force to continue our existence, life after life, after life.

Let us look at the burning candle. Its flame continuously burns but has no physical "entity". It is in a flux. Perceptually a frame of the flame exists for an infinitesimal instant. The next instant, another frame manifests from the previous one, not necessarily of the same hue. The change continues. Transfer of one to the other is smooth but just perceptible if you attune your gaze with awareness. With equanimity you observe impermanence, arising and falling of frame after frame of the flame. Such is the analogy of living as to the burning of the candle. (By sheer chance, the analogy of observing breath in meditation to observing the flame can also be made. In the type of meditation we do here, please note that visualizing a candle or any icon is not allowed; nor verbalizing a mantra.)

Time and space, or instance and frame, are the pillars of relative reality that is the stuff of our existence. It gives us apparent solidity. Let us go behind the "mirror" of "instance and frame" and look back. Zap! We simply cannot comprehend; time and space "confine" us in our concepts.

I remember an experience at one particular meditation session. I was in the middle of the ocean and looking around all I could see was the deep blue sea meeting the light blue sky in a line. I had no feeling of my body; just awareness of me in the middle of the ocean looking at the horizon all around at a distance. Suddenly the line disappeared! It was a feeling of dimensionless ecstasy. I do not know how long that feeling lasted; it seemed only a few seconds. I never had that experience again. I know that if I expect it, however subtly, it will never happen.

There I go again! Fantasizing!

It is important to understand that all the detailed imagery, the usage of the analogy of a burning candle and "insightful" phenomena is an attempt to explain difficult concepts. We are limited in our day-to-day life to explain the experiences developed in practicing meditation. Each meditator's experience is unique; yet there are general common strands.

Regular practice enhances one's understanding of indescribable absolute reality. Also many aspects of living become easier to deal with; one develops an ability to see through the fallacy without getting emotionally involved.

All the religions pretty well agree on the mode of conduct to live our lives.

❂ What are your thoughts about code of conduct and morality? Please write them down. **(30)**

The best way to conduct your life is to ask this question: "Would not I like to be treated the same way as I treat others?"

This would automatically dispense off killing, stealing, lying and adultery. It also behooves us to respect the laws of the society we live in, neighbourly relations, paying taxes, queuing for limited resources, donating time and/or money to the needy, casting your votes and doing your civic duty. Should the "system" malfunction, after in-depth analyses, you should endeavour to correct it legally and, importantly, peacefully.

In meditation, we purify the mind. Alcohol tends to clutter our thinking; it is counterproductive. Smoking cigarettes and using drugs are also not conducive to wellness of mind (and body). Eating meat, fish and anything that has potency for life (eggs) is not proper because of the precept of not killing. Any encouragement to killing is also taboo; that means buying from a butcher or a shop does not absolve one from abetting in the act of killing. However, should the animal have died of natural causes, no life is presumed to have been taken.

Above are the obvious guidelines to form the basis of good living. There may be situations, such as euthanasia, abortion, capital punishment, etc., that are out of scope for us; contentious issues and personal beliefs are best dealt with in each individual circumstance. Perhaps a good sitting at meditation may shed light on your particular dilemma.

We have built a solid platform for a life to be lived well. Neither burdensome nor quarrelsome, we are compassionate and helpful. We dispense a good dose of humour. We live in moderation and always take the middle way in every endeavour. With a zest for life, we continue.

Karma means action. The result of it bears fruit, phal. Accidentally drop a hammer and the toe hurts, ouch! However, if you deliberately hit some one with the hammer, both cause and effect take place in the mind. Any premeditated action of body, speech or mind results in the corresponding fruit of it in the mind; volition determines the nature of the fruit.

A dacoit kills a traveller, stabbing him with a knife. A surgeon removes a cancerous tumour; but the patient dies. Volition of the dacoit was unwholesome while that of the surgeon was full of compassion even though a knife was used and the result was same in both cases.

When one commits a crime in anger, for example, he feels burning sensations, hard breathing and rapid heart beat. Tremendous mental agitation is felt by the heinous act. It creates a damning impression for a lifetime and more. Carrying such a tortuous mind is a punishment, even if one makes light of the crime.

At its basic level, at the aggregation of the vibrations (we talked about previously), there are four elements: earth, air, water and fire. Depending upon the mind's disposition at any given instant, the person "feels" heaviness, windiness, fluidity or heat. Actually the feeling is a mixture of all with a preponderance of a particular predominant one. If anger ensues, for example, the fire element is predominant, raising the sensation of heat. In the mind, unbeknownst to the perpetrator of the crime, a deep crevice is formed.

Such is the working of karma, volition and its fruit, immediately dispensing justice in proportion to the crime. Again, because of one's ignorance, one may not heed to or feel it. The chasm created in the psyche of the mind brings ruin to the culprit. Also a good deed brings about the feeling of warmth. The breathing is also affected by excitement.

Mind feels elated. But be careful, ego may take the credit for it! Then the protrusion created in the psyche of the mind brings ruin again by self-importance. (Of course chasm and protrusion are just conceptions of imagery.) However, if a good deed is done without any expectations and without stroking our ego, the mind is at ease and peaceful. Thus the purpose of life is apparent; just be good.

We deduced that out of nothing we are created in a continuum of existence. What then is the meaning of life? Who knows? One thing is certain -that we are here to experience "something". While we are at it, we might as well celebrate and try to make the best of our lot.

With the above precepts and understanding the law of cause and effect let us lead a full life.

An artist passionately paints a beautiful picture. A craftsman meticulously chisels a perfect idol. A poet magically arouses the ardor of love through a tapestry of poetry. A dancer skillfully moves in rhythmic gyrations. A musician enchantingly transforms the airwaves. A writer evocatively draws imagery of faraway places and eclectic characters. A singer soothingly sings in a melodious voice. A playwright dramatically portrays the plot of a story. An actor profoundly conveys the portrait of a character.

Where are you, in the above canvas of life?

A doctor, an engineer, a lawyer, a pilot, an accountant…

What are you doing in the landscape of life?

A father, mother, brother…

Who are you in the fabric of life?

Soccer, football, hockey, cricket, volleyball…

Piano, accordion, flute….

Oh the latte…

Italian, Indian, Greek, Mexican, languages, cuisines and cultures…

Aroma of the cinnamon buns...

Mozart, Beethoven, Bach, Verdi…
Leonardo Da Vinci, Michael Angelo, Monet….
Mona Lisa, Sistine Chapel, Lilies…
The Blue Danube, Moonlight sonata….

Shakespeare, Dickens, Tennyson…
Romeo and Juliet, Tale of Two Cities, melancholy…

Childhood memories, sweet heart, high school prom, college...
"Twinkle, twinkle little star…"

The smell of the earth after a light rain…

The shining diamonds floating on the vast lake in slanting rays…

Gardening, carpentry, collecting stamps, pictures…

Life is an oyster – la dolce vita.

In a cosmopolitan city one can take an Irish girl to an Italian restaurant owned by Greek, seated by a Chinese and served by Vietnamese in French. A diverse ethnic band plays assorted music from around the world. What a life!

Life is a mosaic of activity. It is an opportunity to create, to express, to feel and most importantly to live. Make each day count as if it is the last one in this life. Vicissitudes in life are bound to be there, so face the challenges with rectitude.

Every success has a seed of failure; every failure is an aspiration to succeed, such is the mode of life, forever flowing by momentum. You have the chance to alter its course; let it be to your advantage.

The Time/space continuum enforces us to think in concepts: duality, solidity, feeling, etc. A concept is a "vessel" to hold the flavour of an idea, scent of a flower - indescribable. This sentence itself is a concept. Concepts may drag you down the ruinous path if the ego convinces us of our "invincible" self and wants us to secure forever "better" conditions. We can change the script to better our life. Yes we can.

At the start of this journey our mind was like a record stuck in a groove; nonstop chatter of runaway demands by every input to the mind. We observed it dwelling on past and future, never in present. Mind seems to be afraid of the present moment; perhaps we may "see" through the veil of deception, of permanence. As time went by in our journey, our chatter was always there but there were moments of "seeing" through the veil. As we practice meditation, we increase the duration and intensity of our experience of the reality of impermanence. We are still making use of concepts to understand the Truth.

At this point, let me venture to fast forward our experience to the last concept, which we discard at the realization of the Truth. This is my conceptual scenario of "awakening". I have not reached there. Nor do I strive to reach there. I simply meditate, doing nothing special.

This, then, is the last scenario at the vortex of inversion, concept of awakening:

One feels himself like an ocean - with placidity of stillness and profundity of depth. Calm and collected, one's heart feels compassion for all, soothingly flowing out. Light and transparent, one is suffused with the Universe. At this last concept, the line of the "horizon" disappears!

 "Chandu, you have a wild imagination!" said my teacher.

Did I fool you again, oh striver of the Truth? You have only to meditate and not let anyone, but anyone, confuse you with antics, semantics or romantics, not even by your fleeting mind.

Life is full of episodes that may lift your spirits high or tumble you down low. Both are important to experience the human life. Understanding the laws of impermanence and karma, one practices meditation to make one's own future bright. Meditation, in turn, makes one further understand these laws.

Oh seeker of Truth, did we reach our signpost? What are your thoughts on the subject of life and how to lead it? **(31)**

Chapter 7
3-STAR HOTEL

This is a very special resort. Here we will consolidate all our learning, our striving.

At the beginning, there was confusion of the mind: we had felt misery. We looked for a reason for it. We found that desire locks us in a forever wanting to possess and perform, while the reality of impermanence dictates otherwise. Not knowing this truth, we keep striving aided and abetted by our ego down the slippery slopes of misery. Luckily, we found that there is a way out of misery – meditation.

It was done by peeling off a layer of the mind's confusion. It is scientifically proven that there is no solidity; everything is in a flux. My body, my mind and my being (consciousness) are all, at an elemental level, existing continually through the repeated process of becoming. This "becoming" is a drive to continue. The sum product of this process gives us apparent solidity. This in itself is not a bad thing; it is the essence of our life. We are blessed with, especially in human form, the ability to intelligently investigate our predicament. We might as well enjoy a "full" life, adjusting our ways to the lessons learnt in our search.

The solidity, unfortunately, gives rise to ego. Out of an initial vast calm and deep ocean of life, so to speak, a ripple breaks out and "sees" itself as a separate independent entity. This culminates into a wave of ego by protecting its newfound existence. Desire, fuelled by grasping for the things to its liking and detesting things it hates, demands more and better things eternally. Thus desire boosts ego to a tsunami. "I" want this and not that. Deep tracks are etched in the mind. These tracks build a persona; a set of varied characteristics that defines "one". Like an oxen cart stuck in the track, one is helplessly mired in one's traits of personality. Following the karmic law of cause and effect, very deeply etched tracks or chasms drive the consciousness to "becoming". We are thus trapped in a vicious cycle of birth and death.

There are three types of tracks. One drawn in water disappears instantaneously. One drawn on the beach is erased by a wave. But one chiseled in stone stays for a long time. Thus some memories are embedded for a lifetime. It is said that the most profound "etched" memory at the time of death dictates the next life.

The mind, like a wild horse, can be slowly trained to cut through the clouds of confusion and see the underlying calm ocean, inherently within us. Even a few glimpses of the ocean make us confident of our search and direction. The journey we embarked upon, ironically, actually goes backwards towards where we must have started from eons ago!

It is amazing that meditation, without any analysis or concepts, sees through the layer of confusion. We witness the mind's play-acting without "our-self". We are no longer "creating" our world; we see reality as it is and not as we like it to be. Then we do not have to fight uphill to keep up the façade of our creation.

We have to empty our minds of any thinking; just observe the breath and the sensations in a small area to keep our mind in the present moment. Patiently, we observe sensations with awareness and equanimity. We are alert and we know that sensations will pass away (impermanence) without us getting tangled up with them. This is simple but requires lots of practice. Surprisingly, as we practice meditation, the more and more we feel "at home" deep within us.

Meditation is carried into our daily activities and in our contemplating reflections. Any process, such as preparing meals, gardening, walking, eating, bathing, etc., are to be done with mindfulness of every aspect in subtle detail. Now and then, it is worthwhile to waste a good hour or two to watch the clouds, falling snow or rain, the mountain or lake, rolling waves, traffic from the window, etc. Such activities arrest one in the present moment and soothe the mind.

To sharpen the mindfulness, it is also recommended that we get out of mediocrity and slothfulness. We take a different route to work. We make an effort to specifically congratulate someone who has done a good job and to help one who is going through a rough time. We are, of course, grateful. We are not inhibited; we do some things differently. Have you ever walked in pouring rain on a hot summer day? A good hot shower after your walk will amazingly refresh you. It also gives a different perspective to life. How about doing something on the spur of the moment? Maybe drive to the airport just to have a coffee. While there, watch the people in a hurry to catch their plane, saying goodbyes to loved ones. How about dancing to Bolero? Singing at the top of your voice with zest and gusto? What about climbing a tree or going on a swing? Childish? If you don't do these now, it may be too late one day.

The world is your oyster. Enjoy!

We have come to a very important and special relationship. Now we are equal partners in our journey. I apologize if I sounded condescending and I deeply regret if you were offended. I have a lot to learn.

We must be regular in meditation with its attendant awareness and equanimity; and be mindful in our activities. Like training a wild horse, we emphasize patience, discipline and compassion in our approach.

After having whetted your appetite for the journey, I recommend you take a formalized meditation course, if you've not already done so. There are many types of meditation and many different courses within each type. I have full confidence that you will find something to your liking, suiting your personality. Also there are a plethora of books on Buddhism to enrich your wisdom. The search for both the right meditation course and for selective reading is in itself an invaluable and rewarding journey, as alluded to in the preface of collecting treasures in the Scouts' game. Good luck!

Of course there are no more lessons and no more signposts, partner.

⊛ Please comment on every aspect of the journey for the last time. **(32)**

From now on, I will continue to express my insights to further chart the way not yet travelled. I will also put forward ideas espoused from diverse readings I have done. You are welcome to join in the research. As before, we can only write what we think is right. We may be wrong.

PART TWO
...THE JOURNEY CONTINUES

Chapter 8
THE MAN, HIS MISSION AND HIS MESSAGE

If there exists a life in which one lived from crib to grave in good health, never got old and had nothing to worry about. Would you like it? It is tempting to say yes. It is like those lithe blonde blue-eyed beach boys chasing slow running lithe blonde blue-eyed girls into the ocean waves. It is a life to be lived for, say, a hundred, nay a thousand years and then just pass away.

Human life, on the contrary, is full of misery. Misery tends one to investigate the cause thereof; the way we did at the start of our journey. Lessons learned on the journey of investigation teach us "something" we would never have learnt without misery. As such misery is our teacher: a great teacher. But what does it teach? What is that "something'? In our journey, we have a feeling that the goal seems to be to see reality as it is; perhaps to go beyond the time and space confine. We humans are endowed with intelligence to find that wisdom if we heed to the impetus driven by misery. No other species have this advantage.

Besides, luckily the life span is short so as not to suffer for a long time. Ironically, though, it gives us a short window of opportunity.

Siddhartha said that human life is a precious jewel. This is how he described how difficult and rare it is:

"Take all the oceans of the world with one turtle swimming in it. Once a century, it comes up to the surface to breath air for a few seconds. Now there is only one necklace floating in the wide ocean. What is the chance of that turtle coming up for fresh air to don on the floating necklace? Such is the probability of acquiring a human life."

Siddhartha was very firm in telling his followers not to believe him; but to empower themselves through meditation to experience the Truth, one's own Truth. He admonished those who blindly followed his words or idolized him. Enquiry is the most precious commodity in searching for Truth.

You heard a lot about a new restaurant that opened in your neighbourhood. Eager to try it out, you take your family to it on the special occasion of your anniversary. There is a long queue. But you know that it is worth the wait. At last you are seated. The menu boasts a variety of your favourite dishes. You look around and see people relishing their meals. You give your order, your mouth watering. At last, the meal is served; the aroma is heavenly. You put the first morsel in your mouth…

No matter what people say (public opinion) or what the menu lists (ads) or, for that matter, how the people around you relish their meal (experts), the real proof is when you taste it. That is your Truth. People may boast about their religious beliefs, special functions at the place of worship may faze you, religious books may entice you and priests may show their vast knowledge; but the proof is in the pudding when you taste it yourself, your own experience.

Siddhartha realized the Truth; he became enlightened. Though it is not our Truth, we are grateful to him for showing the path so we do not have to reinvent the wheel.

Claiming no divinity, Siddhartha Gautama was borne into a well-to-do ruler family of the Sakya clan living at the foot of the Himalayas. Though growing up in comfort and spoilt in princely luxuries, he tended to be pensive and melancholic. After the birth of his child, he felt fettered. He had come to the point of making a crucial decision.

Siddhartha "went forth", i.e. renounced the worldly life, to answer this question:

"Why is there misery in life?"

He was impacted profoundly by observing sickness, old age and death. He realized that he was not exempt from these afflictions even though in good health and, being a prince, living in luxury. He internalized the problem without being morbid. He undertook training in meditation under well-known teachers of his time. After mastering the techniques, he was nowhere near his quest. There was a renaissance of sorts in his time. Not happy with the rigidity of Hinduism, seekers of reality underwent austerities and searched deep within themselves. The strivers, as they were called, roamed the countryside debating, exchanging ideas and coalescing into groups. There was the excitement of a "New Era" offing in the air. The traditional reverence and hospitality of the Indian households enabled the strivers to continue their search unabated. With some of these strivers, Siddhartha undertook the severest of penances to "kill" his ego, as was the custom then to reach enlightenment, to know the Truth. Emaciated, near death, he did not reach his quest, never mind being enlightened.

Like a scientist he abandoned his failed approach against his colleagues' remonstrations. They left him. After months of recuperating and trying to make headway, he had an epiphany! It came to him, very vividly, that when he was a mere child, sitting under a rose-apple tree, one hot summer afternoon while his father's men were ploughing the field, he was suddenly in an ecstatic state of mind. He felt his whole being suffused in the bright sunlight, soaring with energy. What he realized was that that experience had just happened spontaneously. Eureka! He was striving too hard! Let it be! With this insight, he meditated without striving hard: without forced concentration, conceptions or expectations. He simply practiced it freely, naturally.

One full moon night, under a peepal tree, he sat with the determination not to get up without achieving enlightenment – the last push. He meditated through the night and was enlightened in the early morn as the full moon was swathed with the rising sun. Enlightenment means knowing the Truth with eternal "deep-ocean calm" within. No more cloudy, clinging mind; pure serenity. Everyone has this natural mind and everyone is entitled to be enlightened! Then there is no more "becoming", no more self-perpetuating agenda, no more misery; simply indescribable dimensionless, timeless absolute reality. This is not nihilism, not no-thing and not even any-thing; simply bliss not comprehensible on this side of existence. He received no divine dispensation. A human being dove deeply into himself to bring up a pearl of wisdom!

After some weeks of contemplating his achievement, he, out of compassion for sentient beings, espoused his discovery to the world for the rest of his life.

The Buddha, as Siddhartha is called, simply means the enlightened one. You could be one. There were many Buddhas before Siddhartha, many after him and many more to come. His fame and contribution was to share his knowledge; as a teacher of the path he discovered, he is venerated as the supreme Buddha.

He had taken the middle way, neither severe penances nor princely comforts, to achieve his goal. His teachings reflect the Middle Path or Middle Way. His drive, dedication and determination are exemplary to all seekers. His patience and compassion are legendary.

I can only say that my meditation course intrigued me to learn more about him. I felt progress being made in my search. I had read about Buddhism before and did not understand much of it. But after following his meditation techniques, I am collecting seashells at the seashore of the wide ocean of knowledge.

Apart from improving my life, meditation has introduced to me a world of immense insights, not to mention the path itself. What attracted me most was the empowerment given to me in my ever-continuing search, without condescension and with openness.

All Buddha's teachings are based on his experience. Many a time he was asked about God, the soul, the meaning of life, etc. He had to tell the questioner that such things are not profitable to be rid of misery; he only knew that following the path, one would achieve enlightenment; freedom from suffering.

To paraphrase, he said,

"What is the point of asking such questions when you are suffering? If an arrow has pierced your head, would you ask the surgeon what kind of an arrow is it? Is its head made of lead? Is it dipped in poison? You want to stop suffering, period. Besides, I never promised you any such knowledge; all I show is the path to overcome misery".

He had a knack of teaching to the level of the audience. He made a point of teaching in the local vernacular to make sure that people understood his teachings. At times he would, for example, say soul instead of consciousness to get his point across to the followers of a Hindu sect. Yet in front of a well renowned Hindu Brahmin, he would simply not answer questions about the existence or non-existence of the soul because it would lead to conflicting ideas in the mind of the receiver.

In response to the request of simplifying his teachings, the Buddha responded,

"Do wholesome activity, reject unwholesome ones and purify your mind; these are all the Buddhas' teachings."

He was asked why he could not, being so powerful, just eradicate misery from the world. He explained that like anyone else, he had to find his own way. He could not even carry anyone on the path; he can only show the way. Everyone has to follow each step of the path by oneself.

He used practical symbolism to the grieving person to internalize the process and thus accept the reality as it is:

🪷 Gotami would not accept the death of her child; he will soon wake up from his sleep. She went to Buddha so that he may help her give some magic potion to expedite the process. Buddha asked her to bring a few mustard seeds from a household, where no one had died. Gotami wandered for days begging for mustards. Alas, there was not a single household without death. The message was understood. She followed Buddha's dharma to become an Arhant.

🪷 A man would not accept Buddha's words of consolation for his recently departed father.
"Please do some thing for my father to go to heaven."
Buddha asked him to bring two clay pots; one filled with ghee and other with pebbles. He then had the mouths of both the pots covered and tied. They were thrown in the river and Buddha with a stick broke open the pots and started praying,
"Please let the ghee sink down to the bottom and pebbles float up the surface!"
The man was puzzled, "Impossible".
Buddha said,
"That's exactly what I have been telling you! Your father's karma in life dictates his phal in after life."

When asked before his passing away about the fate of Sangha, the order of the monks and nuns to perpetuate Dharma, his teachings, he responded,

"The path of Dharma and the rules for Sangha are well laid out with transparency."

Of all the transcendental knowledge passed on to humankind, Buddha's teachings have only recently been appreciated as a scientific endeavour. His paramount contribution was in experiencing reality directly through meditation, -which happens to be a branch of the science of Yoga. This validates Buddha's prescient uttering, as above. It also shows Buddha's confidence in people's ability to appreciate his teachings and his misapprehension about creating a schism.

Though there are many exquisite legends about the Buddha, he never taught what he had not experienced first hand. So there was no room for error. He was very thorough in his explanations and took pains to elicit questions from listeners. Even before his passing he exhorted the assembled monks and nuns to ask him any questions about the Dharma. When none had any questions, he, given that one may feel shy or intimidated to question him, offered them to ask the question through a neighbour. How considerate!

> A person in queue to view the resting Buddha in his final hours requested Ananda, Buddha's secretary, that the Buddha give him dispensation of Dharma, then and there, since he would not be there next morning. Buddha upon overhearing the argument said,

"Ananda, send him to me. He is the right person to receive Dharma"

Unfortunately, the Buddha's teachings have been viewed through a prism of religion, even though they do not relate to any divinity. Buddha asked no one to give up his or her religion. All through his quest he had foremost in his mind to help human beings alleviate their misery. Enlightenment by its nature makes the person share their experience with the world. Why not? But it takes a Buddha, out of compassion, to show the Path to whomever is inclined to follow it. The only requirement to follow the teachings is breathing; matters it not that it belongs to a Hindu, a Muslim or a Christian; nor does it matter if it is Indian, Greek or Japanese. Of course men and women, old and young, rich and poor of any colour, persuasion or ilk are also included.

Since Buddha's enquiry was the driving force in his quest, Buddhism fully supports any scientific endeavours; if the Earth is a rotating globe revolving around the sun, so be it. Though many aspects of Buddhism concur with recent scientific discoveries in neurology, cosmology, quantum physics and psychology, it ruefully erred in geography, physiology, anatomy, etc. There are no qualms in accepting any reality; previous erroneous beliefs are forthwith discarded. Ever open to new ideas, Buddhism is eternal; evolving to help sentient beings be happy. However, the Middle Path itself is to follow in line with the Universal Law.

It is human nature to exaggerate the works of eminent personage; more so then, over two thousand years ago, in the Indian culture. Needless to say it was easy to weave a tapestry of then current folklore to honour Buddha out of love and devotion. Some stories, though arcane, have nuanced meanings of spiritual truths. Be that whatever it may, the core teachings of Buddha, as mentioned before, are unblemished. Buddhism did, however, acquire the local cultural infusion as it travelled to Tibet, China, Japan, Sri Lanka and to Southeast Asia.

Here I have only touched upon the relevant aspects of Buddhism that influenced my journey. I have learned a lot from reading about Buddha. Through his teachings, I feel him as a mentor by my side. There are a lot of books available to peruse, my dear researcher.

Chapter 9
2-STAR HOTEL

We have come to a very remote place; the world seems afar.

This is actually our good fortune since we need the quietude to meditate and really dive deep into our ocean of knowledge.

First and foremost we meditate….

The hotel is on a vast lake with surrounding mountains sitting like bearded sages contemplating the serenity of the lake. We "smidgens", undaunted, imitate.

Gazing at the far end of the lake transfixed, we feel the shadows of absolute reality in the lifting fog. A ripple in the light breeze turns into a wave with a white crest moving towards the distant fog. A soaring eagle with wings stretched majestically swoops down to the wave and, with a quick projecting of its talons, catches a fish and rises up without losing momentum. The trajectory is completed as it soars up with a shining trophy in its possession.

 "Chandu, you have a wild imagination."

Did I fool you? Sorry, I got carried away.

Seriously, every action of mind, body and speech creates a track, a sankhara, in the mind. These tracks are subliminal, under the radar screen of awareness. The deeper sankharas, the type etched in rock, activate responses to a stimulus causing us to behave in a predictable manner; a habit pattern. In an addict, for example, a trigger starts the process of craving to get a fix. Some sankharas, though, lie dormant deep in the recesses of the mind.

There is also another analogy of sankharas: seeds. Upon receiving the fodder, they germinate, grow and take root in the mind. They multiply as more fodder is received.

In meditation, we observe sensations without reacting to them, and no new ones are formed. Then something wonderful happens: old sankharas come to surface (past memories are aroused) thereby giving us the opportunity to deal with them again. This time we meditate with awareness and equanimity to eradicate them. We feel relieved and light. When all the sankharas are destroyed, there is no more "becoming".

A sage had reached nirvana, a state of "not becoming". In the final seconds of his life, he happened to look up and admire a rose apple. He had to come back as a worm in a rose apple to burn the sankharas developed. There are two lessons learned in this story; the last thought of a life is the progenitor of the future life and all sankharas have to be burnt before nirvana.

What then are the causes of suffering, dukkha? They are the forces (klesha) of attraction (raga), aversion (dvesha) and delusion (maya). Attraction is the thirst (tanha) or hunger of wanting things. Aversion is hatred or fear of things disliked. We covered these in causing sankharas. Delusion is not knowing things as they are: ignorance. Of course, delusion, as we saw, makes us believe in things that do not exist; giving rise to ego.

As we analyzed above, meditation helps us remove the sankharas and see the wide peaceful and deep state of mind that is our true self. In slow motion, as it were, we live the present moment, moment by moment, fully appreciating the resonance with reality. A soprano singer has shattered the glass. A musician is fully attuned to his instrument. A dancer is ecstatic in rhythm. The self merges with the Universe, no more duality, no more time and space. Such is the power of meditation to reverse the process of refraction of colours into a single light; suffused into itself.

We feel the benefits accrued immediately in this life. We do not hanker for the Goal. We simply live to enjoy life with the right attitude and let karma do its work. Let it be!

Did you notice in our journey that the layers of our ignorance were peeled off as the stars of the hotels we stayed in depleted? I wonder what will happen as we reach the hotel with no stars?

Chapter 10
IMAGINE

Imagine a world without theft. No need for locks and no worry of losing a thing! Naive, you say? I am a dreamer.

Imagine a world without killing. No bloodshed and no fear of war. Impossible, you say? I am a dreamer.

Imagine a world without lying. No need to deceive and no worry of being cheated. Crazy, you say? I am a dreamer.

Imagine a world without sexual misconduct. No falsehood and no fear of abuse. Never, you say? I am a dreamer.

Imagine a world without alcohol. No loss of reason and no fear of misbehaving. Won't happen, you say? I am a dreamer.

While you cannot change the world, you can change yourself. Above are the five precepts required to build a solid foundation in living a meaningful life. It is useful to internalize their essence by carefully analyzing the reasons to adopt them. The precept of abstinence from alcohol is to keep the mind clear of impurities. All the other precepts follow the cardinal rule of "do unto others as you would have them do unto you". On further examination it is evident that the best way to improve our karma is to devote our energy to helping others in need. This way, we not only follow the precepts but also build our compassion and automatically improve the society we live in. However, in helping others the onus is on us to carefully judge the merit of the recipients and to balance our involvement. Moreover it is incumbent upon us not to expect anything in return, not even a "thank you" nor any praise.

I have made volunteering one of the main components in my retirement to give structure essential to life. The little things I do go a long way for people in need. I am amazed that I learn so much from people of varied backgrounds and experiences. I am blessed. Needless to repeat the adage "what goes round comes round".

All the afflictions engendered by not following the precepts are the manifestations of the mind. As such a paradigm shift in one, like I, is the most important starting point to better our condition. Knowing the interconnectedness of the Universe, the impermanence of existence and the effect of karma, I can at least make a concerted effort to do no harm. Rather than worry about changing the society over which I have very little control, I can begin with myself with training that comes from meditation. Little by little, further insight is developed by continually diving within myself. As I continue to learn from insights, which manifest themselves automatically, I modify my living from the experience gained. The beneficent cycle continues with myself grounded in joyous living. The cumulative return far exceeds the effort expended. Never losing sight of my humanness, I enjoy my life with the understanding of the limited time at my disposal. I repeat -live!

I am a pragmatist.

Imagine if a populace were to inherently follow the precepts, most manmade problems would disappear in that community.

Now imagine that we add, knowing scientifically and by sound ethical reasoning, the precept of honouring our environment. It makes sense that the very "essence" that supports us needs utmost attention to perpetuate our existence.

Imagine, further, that a potential Einstein or a Mozart or a Michelangelo is snuffed out of existence in poverty when it is within our power to, at least, feed all the children of the world with current technology and resources. Imagine!

Imagine if we contribute our "bit" in the above two precepts, we can help build the world, where you may want to come back perpetually and where hatred is replaced by compassion, war by peace, antagonism by debate and ignorance by learning.

I am a dreamer.

While I know that my paradigm shift will alienate me from the general milieu, I am rather selfish to pursue what I detect to be a golden opportunity to experience the "essence" of life, fully appreciating moment-to-moment, day-to-day. Besides, I do not want to be born, by the law of karma, for example, in the realm of a "hungry ghost" for my greed!

Imagine!

Chapter 11
1.5-STAR HOTEL

We have come to a place, which seems out of this world. We are told by the meager staff of the hotel of some Rishis meditating in the caves yonder in the snow-clad mountains.

The eerie silence is palpable in this remote place – a silence that can be heard louder than thunder in the stillness of the gazillion crisp stars of the night. Enchanted, our minds in cohesion with the magical ambience, we savour the moment. We feel, ever so gently, the slipping away of the moment into another like the lapping of waves on the shore, rhythmically. In the depths of the ocean of our minds, serenity prevails. We are at home.

>   Wearied of travails
>   Tired to the bones
>   Exasperated
>   Alas! We reach Silence
>
>   A home of eternal peace
>   Free of shackles
>   Of time and space
>   Of thoughts
>   Of concepts
>
>   Peace, peace, peace.

❂   A star streaks across the sky, blazing a trail. In awe, I follow its path watching its showery demise. My memory awakens to fire works we as children played with. A rocket shoots up, whistling, above our heads, and explodes with a bang in a multicolour spray of bright particles for a second and dies. Among the shouts of jubilation, another rocket is ignited from across the street. At Deewali, kids form ad hoc gangs to compete in a showmanship of firepower. Starting in a friendly camaraderie, it soon gets fierce with bangers (loud crackers) thrown at each other, not unlike soldiers throwing grenades. Deftly, checking the burning of the fuse, one may pick up and return the banger, timing it to explode as it reaches the other side. Before long, tacitly, undeclared war has developed. Euphoric, in the heat of the moment, the "rockets" are aimed low at each other while dodging the missiles. With bravado, one may light a string of "crackers", run to the enemy camp and throw it, crackling, in their midst. Passionate in our endeavour, we fight with vengeance. With pride in our ability to deftly dodge and to counteract, we friends become enemies; the pungent smell of mortars stinging our nostrils on streets littered with strewn paper.

Even now at the foothills of Himalayas, I shudder at the ease with which the mind jerks one on a roller coaster ride.

Let us try to analyze the mind again. Consciousness, like software, somehow interacts with the brain helping in the process of neural connections: the mind, akin to firmware in computer lingo. Mind and body, in relative reality, are thought of as material, consciousness is without form (brain is the physical part of the body; mind is "wired" with neural connections while consciousness is energy/capacity/essence: the way I understand it). With neural connections established, consciousness also, somehow, helps to give expression to the mind: thought, language and culture. Consciousness, though pulsating, can be thought of as a "stream" flowing in the Universe, life after life after life. Collecting "thought" sediment at the dictates of the mind at every life instant, the consciousness flows according to its "collective" sediment content, muddy and sluggish. The sediments are the afflictions discussed previously – ego with a slew of adjunct passion, hatred, anger, etc. Positive aspects like compassion and love are of sparklingly clear composition in the stream, in proportion to their development.

Nowhere in science is the knowledge of consciousness nailed down in our understanding of the Universe. Who am I to fathom its intricacies? Without any claim to know even an iota of its vast immaterial presence, I speculate through introspection and insight. Above is the gist of such an endeavour, "somehow" being used to underscore my utter ignorance.

☸ In a retreat of a ten-day meditation course, three novices were summoned at a time from the assembled to confirm our understanding of the techniques used. We were seated on the floor in front of the assistant teacher on a dais about a foot high. I was on the right side of the teacher. Each of us was consulted on our individual application and experience of the specific techniques used. In whispers the dialogue continued to correct ones understanding. Before my turn, I had mentally decided not to "bother" him with a subtle point of the technique, thinking that it will sort itself out in coming days. At the end of our discussion, he asked of us,

"Is there anything you want to ask?" scanning from left to right ending with me. No. None of us had.

"Alright, you can go."

All of us started to get up. He motioned waving his right hand across me to stay. I sat down.

"Is something bothering you?" He then explained, patiently, the subtle point I thought insignificant.

This was the merging of our consciousness, he the adept.

Many of us have had an experience that baffles us; is it our imagination? Do some people have higher awareness of body language? Mind reading?

Meditation, introspection and insight lead to wisdom as yet unfathomed by us, ordinary mortals.

In meditation, we endeavour to simply watch our breath, coming in, going out. Discursive thoughts arise. We watch, detachedly. One after the other, they melt away. More come to surface. Patiently, with awareness we watch with equanimity. Without guilt or remorse, we gently focus on the breath at the nostril(s). We watch for the sensations in a small area below nostrils to see them arising and passing with awareness yet detached. The mind gets clearer of the sediment, seeds or sankharas; matters it not whichever concept one uses. There is a long way to go; yet the benefits are felt as we progress. Introspection comes naturally to check the mind's play. Insight follows with detached understanding of the mind, and thereby our universe; our truth.

We continue to develop our awareness in daily activities, thus practically merging our meditation with living – meditation in motion. Tai chi and yoga offer formal settings while activities like cooking, gardening, walking, waiting in a queue and watching any activity (construction sites or soccer, baseball, etc.) give us an opportunity to practice awareness in various ways. We are actually aware of sensations in these activities. When we eat, we eat. Each sensation of each step of the process is minutely felt. Also changing the routine makes one be aware of new ways of looking.

Did you notice that as the stars of the hotels we stayed at diminished, so did our ego?

We will try to expand our horizons with a lot of speculations, as I already started with in this chapter. The journey we commenced at the beginning brought us new dimensions by insight. We continued to broaden that insight knowing that what we learned, nay intuitively experienced, is not fathomable by science or logic. Without apology we continued to break down the barriers, fully understanding our limited resources. Anyone who travels the path, as we do, will no doubt chart his or her own Truth. Never could it be brought under the scrutiny of science, yet it may be worthwhile to compare our notes and perhaps arrive at a consensus. What is Truth?

From now on, I will attempt to put in words sheer speculations, the subjective experience goading me to continue the journey in the fourth dimension, in the quest of understanding consciousness itself.

Chapter 12
1-STAR HOTEL

The hotel we have reached toward the summit of the mountain range is so remote that the only semblance of "civilization" is the fluttering star flag on a tree next to the building: thus the title of this chapter.

We have travelled so far and fortunately we have gotten used to the hardship and importantly our practice in meditation has inured us to accept any situation with a good dose of humour.

Actually, this is a blessing in disguise. We are ready to go to the depths of ourselves to tease out the Truth. What better place than this quiet retreat?

Nothingness Revisited.

Let us go back to the "back" of the mirror – absolute reality.

In life, as experience builds up, our understanding of the Universe changes. We always hold our current position to be valid, with an open mind to accept new ideas albeit with discrimination. We do not erase the past position; in fact, the historical analysis of previous positions gives us a measure of progress and direction – our path to Truth.

We attempted to go behind the mirror from relative to absolute reality. There was no coherence since absolute reality has no dimension and no time frame. We called the other side "nothing" – a concept we can only deal with in relative reality. Let us further our conceptual understanding of "nothing"- the other side. This time let us look back at relative reality from the other side. It becomes immediately apparent that the time/space continuum is a necessary flux to give expression to the dance of existence. Wait a minute; on this side "nothing" is actually essential to support the time/space relative reality! This side is the very basis on which the conditioned assembly of everything occurs on the other side, not unlike a hologram. As such, this side is not nothingness; it is not a void! It is emptiness with a potential to mould and develop. As a matter of fact it is imbued in the relative reality; no need to go to the other side of the mirror. The relative reality, in fact, depends upon this emptiness; it cannot exist without it. The emptiness has "luminosity" and "expanse" to support the relative reality! The "expression" through "experience" of "existence" in relative reality is essential to life. (All quoted words are concepts; so are all the ideas.) Is this a Zen (koan) moment?

Scientists have discovered that certain entangled molecules have left and right spinning properties. When two such molecules are separated by vast space and if one left or right spinning molecule is made to change its rotation, its counterpart reverses its rotation instantly even though millions of miles apart. This defies our current knowledge of science. It may be possible to explain such a phenomenon through the understanding of "emptiness", not to be confused with space. Space is the antithesis of solid material and requires dimensions while emptiness is formless.

In a nutshell, then, everything – materials, ideas, lives, and even consciousness – exists because of the play of conditions and causes thereof. For a pot to exist it needs materials, a craftsman, machinery and a kiln; not to mention the skill, the environment and effort needed to complete the job. Also certain conditions (spouse in a good mood, no upset stomach, etc.) have to be present (or absent) for a successful job. All aspects of the process have to be met. Similarly, all underlying conditions have to be met for a hologram or for anything to "exist".

The cruel irony is that everything exists, though "created" from no inherent "components", because of the interdependence of facilitating conditions. This assessment solidifies our understanding of impermanence, continuous flux with no substance. Though "material" things have "flowed" from the inception of the "Big Bang" (perhaps from earlier incarnation), formless consciousness eludes its origins.

The understanding of the relation between relative and absolute realities is fundamental in our journey to the Truth. It gives a bird's eye view of our existence. We need not be bogged down with the mundane aspects of life. We see the interconnectedness of "everything". We realize the importance of the opportunity afforded to achieve our goal especially in human form, being endowed with wisdom (i.e. differentiated intelligence) and learning lessons from "suffering". We appreciate the precious gift of life.

What is the goal? Why not take Pascal's view that, given the circumstances of our existence and not knowing the purpose thereof, one should aim for the least damage inducing option. Neumann opted for a least losing, rather than a winning, strategy in his assessment of risk management. Famously, the Hippocratic oath taken by graduating physicians entrenches the philosophy of "do no harm". Life thus has to be lived with an understanding of taking the middle way in our endeavours and with the continual scrutinizing of our actions by the introspection developed through meditation.

In the eventual analysis, live an enjoyable life with due respect to the law of karma, savouring every moment of life.

Chapter 13
GROUND ZERO

Now here is the deal.

You are here. You don't know where you came from or where you are going. You have no clue, whatsoever, of what you are doing! Absolutely clueless!

Let us try to understand your predicament.

Author's note: This chapter is extremely important to a serious reader, who considers going deeper in his search for truth. It is important to realize that every one interprets the truth in one's own way. The following ideas are my own understanding of reality; part of it is intuitively experienced but mostly from a plethora of Buddhist materials available to the public. The reader is welcome to go though his own research. The subject matter varies in its complexity, from mundane to profound; the deepest level, being speculative, requires a lot of reflections. I also feel that I am taking advantage, selfishly, of this opportunity to present my take on the issue of "existence" for my own clarity and, of course, for posterity.

On the way to work, you are rushing, with a horde of commuters, not unlike elephants on a rampage, to make it in time for the weekly review meeting you have not had time to prepare for; your one year-old kid was running high fever overnight and you tended to him and your wife has taken time off today to take him to the pediatrician. You have winged it in such meetings many times before. As usual you will be late by at least five minutes. All around you, you see people tense like pressure cookers about to explode. Only last week a woman commuter had splashed a hot coffee on the face of a guy she thought cut her off at Union station! You walk like a zombie into your office building saying pleasantries to your colleagues, not meaning a single word.

Such a plastic existence! Oh, how you hate your job? Same routine! Writing software and playing politics with clowns!

When your wife is too busy with the kids, you are frustrated and get angry easily. The household chores, once manageable, are becoming cumbersome and you take solace in a few drinks at night to counter the wife's nagging. Life seems to have lost its luster; worse – you have lost control! You don't even have time to think! You are in an automatic mode of existence – a robot. Looking in a mirror, you are staring at a stranger.

Let us try to get perspective on our understanding of the situation. First, let us gather what we know.

If you happen to get rather depressed, re-read chapter six on "Joie de Vivre" to pep up. Contemplate on each idea to realize, in your bones, the veracity of reality as it is. I am emphasizing the rotten side of the deal to empower you to grab the bull by the horns.

We are a bag of bones and sinews; of blood, sweat and saliva; of urine and excrement. Any imbalance in our hormones, neural connections, digestion, etc., creates havoc in our system. We are wired with a built-in desire to procreate, as if pulled by the nose in the name of pleasure! Old age creeps in on us, making us vulnerable to all sorts of ailments. We are at the mercy of our environment to sustain us.

Also, our minds are on a roller coaster ride day and night; no peace. We do not have time to think things through. We always think that once we get certain aspects of our life organized we will be in a position to take control. We wish! Subconsciously, we continuously seek our habitual comfort zone. The jarring incidence of a funeral of a relative or a friend so graphically underscoring impermanence, subsides in a few days. Not understanding the reality of this ubiquitous suffering, we strive for happiness by seeking solace in worldly solutions.

I am on a roll here to churn out our negative aspects to drive home the unsatisfactoriness of our existence. I would like to jar you out of the complacency of mediocrity to sensitize your feelings for reality.

Somebody called "I" glares at the world from somewhere behind the eyes. Or is "I" behind the head? And boy, does that "I" have an ego! It swaggers, throwing weight around. It demands the best for what it thinks it deserves. Who am I? Where am I?

We are here without knowing why, how, for how long and what is in store even in the next instance! Sickness may strike any time; old age is around the corner; and death- ahem -happens to others before it touches us; a long way off. It seems we do not have any choice! There is no guarantee we will lead our life in a comfortable state even if endowed with health, wealth and power. Things we like, we do not get enough of or lose them. Things we dislike tend to cling to us. In frustration we manifest pride, jealousy, hatred, anger, desire, etc., in trying to validate our existence; to assert our "I". We are caught, to give an analogy, in a spider's web. The more we try to wiggle out, the more we get entangled!

Fortunately, human life is a tremendous opportunity to escape from the web. Though we are not at the centre of Universe, we occupy a centrist position in six realms of existence according to Buddhist thought. Above are Devas (godlike; exhibiting karmic result of excessive pride) and Asuras (semi-gods; jealousy) with long life spans and without pain, thus lacking incentive to investigate reality. Below are animals (ignorance), hungry ghosts (greed) and hell dwelling creatures (hatred), lacking discriminative enquiry.

Human existence is the only realm that has a reasonable life span and a capacity to decipher the unsatisfactoriness of existence. It is like a lotus plant growing in a turbid pond depicted by negative aspects of our existence. The lotus has the possibility to flower and grow above the pond. This is why a human life is a very precious endowment to enable us to extricate ourselves from the web.

Chapter 14
THE 4ᵀᴴ DIMENSION

It pains me to think of family and friends I may have hurt by my candid description of events leading to the journey; my sincere apologies to them all. Looking back, I can say that the cause of the happenstance was solely my responsibility. A snob, I had a big ego, ever so righteous and demanding. I was angry very often. I smoked, drank regularly and worked hard; deadly recipe for creating tension and ill health.

In retrospect, I feel sorry for Usha, my ex-wife, who had to put up with me. I am also thankful to her for her courage to make a difference. We are good friends now. Of course, there is a price to for such an upheaval for all concerned. Neel and Ravi, our kids, have managed to bear the brunt in their late teenage years. I am grateful to them for navigating those early years admirably. As time went by, each helped one another through. Life goes on. Relatives and friends pitched in to smooth the rehabilitation. The journey...

It is cliché to say that without this, this book would not be here.

What is the book's message?

Simply meditate! Practicing with diligence, one is freed from the conditionality of being trapped in the vicious cycle of suffering.

Appendix A (II) defines the "Conditional Genesis" from life to life. Sensations condition desire [step (7)] without seriously realizing its impact. It is the weak link to be observed with awareness and equanimity. It is important to understand the Four Noble Truths to address Ignorance [step (1)]. This leads one to practice meditation to observe the inputs of the senses from a distance, without getting tangled in desire.

And finally, we reach our conclusion - your journey in the 4th dimension! This journey is a personal trip to the Truth. But first, as promised, let us consider the four dimensions from a new perspective. As mentioned previously, Time is traditionally considered the fourth dimension, other three being spatial. New dimensions can be considered from a standpoint of Sansara, the continuous birth and death cycle:

1st dimension: parents conceiving Life, to procreate.
2nd dimension: a child taking rebirth, through desire to live Life.
3rd dimension: the experience of living Life, fraught with suffering, illness and aging.
4th dimension: the escape from Sansara. Meditating allows one to fully understand Reality, thereby gaining freedom from the routine existence of Sansara.

I hope you enjoy your journey!

APPENDIX A

THE BUDDHA'S TEACHINGS

Presented here is my interpretation of the Buddha's core teachings pertaining to the book.

The Buddha describes what constitutes a "being" (I), how the "being" continues (II), and laws governing the "being" (III).

I. The Five Aggregates: Mind-body Energy forces that constitute a "Being"

Buddha posited that a "being" is composed, in totality, of five aggregates: matter, sensation, perception, mental formations and consciousness. Each of these individually, though in synchrony, pulsates like waves.

(1) The aggregate of matter comprises of solidity, fluidity, heat and motion with properties of expansion, cohesion, temperature and displacement. For sentient beings, five sense faculties (eye, ear, nose, tongue and skin) and their corresponding sense objects (form, sound, odour, taste and tactility) along with sixth mental faculty with thought as its object form the basis of existence. The thought draws on the experiences of the sense faculties, improvises and forms a platform for the play of other aggregates.

(2) The aggregate of sensation has pleasant, unpleasant or neutral feelings. When a sense organ, its related object and its consciousness come together, a sensation arises. Each person feels differently from others depending upon his personality. He may also feel differently under different circumstances. Also each contact may elicit different

feelings of an object from different sense organs; pleasant to the eyes may not be so for the tongue. The mind similarly simulates contact through thought and mind-consciousness.

(3) The aggregate of perception recognizes a sense object (physical or mental) as distinct from others. As such, this distinctive ability brings about a repertoire of memory. The recognition aspect generates evaluation, judgment or belief depending upon upbringing, inhibitions, culture, etc. Perception is, thus, usually contrived and convoluted without any semblance to reality.

(4) Mental formations or volitional actions, good or bad (such as compassionate or hateful, wise or ignorant, etc.), bring about karma (actually karma-phal or effect; colloquially the usage of the term is mixed), charting a future map of the "being". Like all other aggregates, volition is directed to six sense (including mental) objects. It must be understood that the mental formations are willful as opposed to knee-jerk, non-voluntary sensation and perception aggregates. The intention, as in criminal law, holds the sway of the retribution meted out. However, in Buddhism, the karma is not fatalistic since it is in the power of the "being" to negate it by doing good deeds.

(5) Consciousness provides awareness of the "contact" of senses with their respective objects. It, like all other aggregates, fluctuates from moment to moment. In fact, it depends upon arising of and intermixed with other aggregates.

To emphasize "emptiness" of the aggregates, the Buddha described form to sponge, emotions to bubbles, perceptions to mirage, mental formations to plantain plant and consciousness to illusion.

The interplay of the aggregates is how life is lived - fired on all five cylinders - every moment, importantly, fuels the next moments: samsara cycle. The following is an example of how an eye, one of the six senses, affects a "being".

On "seeing" a form (say a sexual object), eye/form/eye-consciousness abide: contact. Sensation arises with a good (tingling) or bad feeling. The awareness of the form triggers recognition in perception (ah! beautiful). Mental, verbal and/or physical reaction(s) follow depending upon the volition of the person (leave it to your imagination). The reactionary karmic seeds (desire for repeats) dictate the future state. The working of the "being" is in correspondence to "Conditioned Genesis" as stated below.

II. "Conditional Genesis" of continuity of life:

This is the fundamental aspect of our flow of existence, life after life: samsara. A "being's" craving for existence through ignorance propels one to continue going round and round, birth and death: a beginning-less cycle.

(1) Ignorance conditions volitional actions or karma formations.

Ignorance here means not understanding the Truths (section III). The karma formations or "characteristic" tendencies of a "being" are based upon her ignorance.

(2) Volitional actions condition consciousness.

The volition in our actions dictates the "make up" of consciousness. The karmic seeds of craving, for example, are imbued in the consciousness to sprout in future.

(3) Consciousness conditions mind-body phenomena.

The state of the consciousness or the latent potency of the karmic seeds in the consciousness dictates the acquisition of the mind and body.

(4) Mind-body phenomena conditions six faculties (five sense organs and mind).

(5) Six faculties condition contact.

(6) Contact conditions sensation.

(7) Sensation conditions desire.

(8) Desire conditions craving.

(9) Craving conditions the process of becoming.

(10) Process of becoming conditions rebirth.

The predominant thought of the mind at the last moment of previous life dictates the state of the present birth: the moment continues but the physical form changes.

The conditional steps 4 to 10 are discussed in previous section of Five Aggregates.

(11) Rebirth conditions (12) aging, death, lamentation, pain, grief, despair. Thus whole gamut of suffering arises. This is called the Noble Truth of the arising of the suffering or Dukkha.

It must be understood that all above conditions are dependent and cyclical; there is no first cause. Life is a continuous flux of mind-body energies. Skillful removal of cause and condition ceases the momentum of the cycle.

III. Four Noble Truths

When one goes to a doctor, ailment is diagnosed, its cause is ascertained, its remedy is found and medication is prescribed. In the same way, the Buddha, endowed with the hindsight of his Enlightenment, declared the four Truths:

(1) There is Dukkha in life
(2) There is a reason for it
(3) There is a way out
(4) This is the way

It is said that all Buddha's teachings are a reflection of Four Noble Truths, the very first discourse given to five strivers and starting Sangha, a community of monks or nuns.

(1) Suffering in life is palpable. We feel it in many ways but we do not quite grasp why. We become accustomed to it. Thus without understanding its significance, i.e. not recognizing the un-satisfactoriness in life, the other three steps are lost. Without extreme pessimism (nihilism) or optimism (eternal), we see reality as it is. A solution can only be found once we know a problem exists. Unfortunately, we have tunnel vision till we come in contact with Dharma…

(2) Craving is the reason for suffering. It keeps the world going; a motivating force in the round of existence with its inherent unsatisfactoriness. The cycle of samsara continues. Craving, as in the "Conditional Genesis", is conditioned, dependent and relative. If only we realize that sense objects, being impermanent, cause misery...

(3) The liberation is achieved by eliminating craving: nirvana, enlightenment, Absolute Truth. This concept is indescribable. The Buddha himself said that it is deep, hard to see and beyond mere reasoning for people delighting and rejoicing in sensual pleasures. When one experiences total annihilation of defilements, one realizes true happiness as never before and yet one can never make others understand it. Enlightened, one knows that at the passing of the body, all feelings will become "cool" just as the fuel runs out extinguishing the oil lamp...

(4) The way is the Noble Eightfold Path

This is the way leading to the cessation of Dukkha. It is known as the "Middle Path" since it avoids extremes: sensual pleasures and self-mortification. All the eight components are to be followed simultaneously aiding each other to strengthen the practice of deliverance. They are also categorized in disciplining as: (a) Ethical Conduct (iii, iv and v), (b) Mental Discipline (vi, vii and viii), and (c) Wisdom (i and ii).

i) Right Understanding

Right Understanding is the understanding of the law, i.e. the Four Noble Truths. We generally grasp knowledge intellectually from reading and listening. We also intuitively understand ethics, cause and effect, and the Truths at a cursory level. But the true penetration, seeing reality in its true nature, is possible when the mind is freed from impurities through meditation. Then the insight is developed to see the clinging of the five aggregates; i.e. realizing our own "being". The five aggregates are impermanent, thereby unsatisfactory and without Self. We experience Truths through meditation and contemplation, not through blind belief, speculation or respect to authority or tradition.

ii) Right Thought

Right thought is the result of Right understanding. Together both these comprise Wisdom. Right thought is renunciation, goodwill and compassion. When lust, as an example of sense stimulant, arises in the mind, one must try to look at it objectively at its origin; its cause. One then cultivates renunciation when understanding that obsession with lust fuels craving. Right thought, then, in this case, is renunciation, an antidote for lust.

iii) Right Speech

Speech is powerful in that it expresses thoughts and ideas. If not controlled, it can bring ruin to oneself. Lies, slanders, harsh words and idle talk are harmful to oneself and others. Noble silence is golden when one is not sure of the repercussions of loose talk.

iv) Right Action

It is abstinence from killing, stealing and sexual misconduct. This builds character as it requires constant vigilance and ethical behaviour. Since it is developed by one's own striving, through exertion and restraint, one reaps merits and improves karma.

v) Right Livelihood

It entails not harming others. Dealing in arms, intoxicants, poisons, killing animals, etc., is forbidden. This promotes happiness, prosperity and unity in individuals, families and nations.

The above three constitutes Ethical Conduct.

vi) Right Effort

The Buddha's last words were, "Subject to change are all component things. Strive on with heedfulness". Striving implies mental energy and determination. Knowing the limited time we have in this life, one continuously makes an effort to

a) Prevent arising of evil thoughts.
b) Abandon the evil thoughts already arisen.
c) Develop mindfulness, Dhamma, energy, emphatic joy, calm, concentration and equanimity.
d) Maintain factors developed in c).

vii) Right Mindfulness

It is awareness of the a) activities of the body, b) sensations, c) activities of the mind, and d) thoughts, concepts and Dhamma. It sharpens the power of observation aiding wisdom: thought and understanding. It keeps the "eye on the ball" discriminating right from wrong in every endeavour.

viii) Right Concentration

This is the meditation of four absorptions:

a) Abandoning passionate desires, sloth, worry, restlessness and doubt, one develops feelings of joy and happiness.
b) Suppressing intellectual activities, one develops tranquility and one-pointed concentration and retaining joy and happiness.
c) Discarding feeling of joy, one remains equanimous.
d) Only equanimity and awareness remain.

To understand the defilements of lust, hate and delusion, one meditates watching the breath to calm the mind and watching the sensations to observe the phenomena of reality. Insight reveals impermanence, suffering and no-self of all conditioned things. It, in turn, leads to Reality, the Four Noble Truths.

The last three factors constitute Mental Discipline, to train and develop the mind.

The efficacy of the path is succinctly explained by the Buddha, "The Dhamma leads to disenchantment, to dispassion, to cessation, to peace, to direct knowledge, to enlightenment, to Nibbana".

Of course, above is a very concise synopsis of the Buddha's teachings. It is hoped that the reader's appetite is awakened to research on his own.

APPENDIX B

A TREATISE ON "NO-SELF"

Our "being", in totality, is a play of five aggregates as explained in Appendix A. The Buddha searched for an enduring entity thro' all five aggregates, insides and outsides, without success. So who is in charge of this phenomenon? No one is. As explained, it is the continuum of a moment-to-moment process of cause and effect fuelled by "craving". The law of impermanence dictates that each of these aggregates, separately yet in concordance, fluctuates and manifests dependant upon underlying causes and conditions, ad infinitum. Then who experiences this phenomenon? A "being" does (by sheer belief of personifying the process) but has no "self".

The notion of "no-self" is the hardest to grasp because of our ingrained cultural inhibitions. We are so much addicted to the soul theory that it would take a lot of clear insights, with patience and wisdom, to grow out of it. The mere belief in soul gives one the comfortable feeling of belonging, validity and continuity: a colossal addiction. As such it requires a humongous paradigm shift in our understanding of reality. First we lost our Earth as the center of the Universe, then our belief of ourselves as the epitome of creation. Now we are to accept that there is no soul (and by extension no creator: no First Cause)!

Ego, a.k.a. supreme "I", takes advantage of our belief in "self" to weave its web. Ego is a mental construct. Once we understand this phenomenon, though, we are on our way to freedom. Since there is no "self" to minister to, the inherent burden of carrying the façade of "I" is released. Fear, greed, jealousy and all the negative afflictions do not make sense. All the negative attributes are replaced by positive ones to extricate us from the web.

ABOUT THE AUTHOR

I was born in Africa in the town of Tabora, in Tanzania. Many Indian families had immigrated there as entrepreneurs. The community was honest and hardworking, fitting in well with the African farmers. As one of the youngest in a family of ten siblings, I quickly learned that I would have to be shrewd to get my fair shake in the family!

As a child, I vividly remember sneaking off to the nearby mountains without letting our parents know. Sometimes we would encounter snakes and alligators on our trips. As students, schooling was always secondary to playing soccer in the streets, using footballs made with our own expertise. We fought to claim that the ball went between the stones marking the goal. These childhood experiences prepared me well for adulthood. After completing secondary school, my family suggested that I should go to London, England, for further studies. My spirits soared, dreaming of life in such a fantastic city. I felt tremendous trepidation to go, however—would I long for family and the comforts of home life? I was one of the pioneers to leave our small town for a foreign country.

I obtained a bachelor's degree in Electrical Engineering from London University, followed by a master's degree from Waterloo University in Canada. Marriage and family life ensued. Over the years I read profusely, trying to understand the meaning of life. Scientific DVDs and books especially attracted me to analyze the Universe.

A sudden incident in my life drew me to research meditation techniques. I practiced many types of meditation to fit my character.

I realized that the most important meaning of life is that the ordained difficulties are to teach you your reality! It is your task to positively handle it.

www.ingramcontent.com/pod-product-compliance
Lightning Source LLC
LaVergne TN
LVHW041640060526
838200LV00040B/1656